W9-ATJ-427

organize now!
YOUR MONEY, BUSINESS & CAREER

organize now!
YOUR MONEY, BUSINESS & CAREER

Jennifer Ford Berry

BETTERWAY HOME
CINCINNATI, OHIO
WWW.BETTERWAYBOOKS.COM

Organize Now! Your Money, Business & Career. Copyright © 2011 by Jennifer Ford Berry. Manufactured in China. All rights reserved. No part of this book may be reproduced in any form or by any electronic or mechanical means including information storage and retrieval systems without permission in writing from the publisher, except by a reviewer who may quote brief passages in a review. The content of this book has been thoroughly reviewed for accuracy. However, the author and publisher disclaim any liability for any damages, losses or injuries that may result from the use or misuse of any product or information presented herein. It's the

purchaser's responsibility to read and follow all instructions and warnings on all product labels. Published by Betterway Home, an imprint of F+W Media, Inc., 10150 Carver Road, Blue Ash, Ohio, 45242. (800) 289-0963. First Edition.

Other fine Betterway Home books are available from your local bookstore and online suppliers. Visit our website at www.betterwaybooks.com.

15 14 13 12 11   5 4 3 2 1

ISBN 978-1-4403-1025-6

Distributed in Canada by Fraser Direct
100 Armstrong Avenue
Georgetown, Ontario, Canada L7G 5S4
Tel: (905) 877-4411

Distributed in the U.K. and Europe by F&W Media International, LTD
Brunel House, Forde Close, Newton Abbot, TQ12 4PU, UK
Tel: (+44) 1626 323200, Fax: (+44) 1626 323319
E-mail: enquiries@fwmedia.com

Distributed in Australia by Capricorn Link
P.O. Box 704, S. Windsor NSW, 2756 Australia
Tel: (02) 4577-3555

Edited by Jacqueline Musser; designed by Clare Finney;
production coordinated by Mark Griffin

Photo by Klix Photography

ABOUT THE AUTHOR

Jennifer Ford Berry is a life organization expert. She has been professionally helping people get their lives organized, both internally and externally, since 2002. She frequently speaks to groups and businesses on various organizing topics. Jennifer is a graduate of Florida Atlantic University in Boca Raton, Florida. She is also the co-owner of Mothertime Marketplace, a huge semi-annual event for moms and children to clear their outgrown clutter for cash.

Jennifer currently resides in western New York with her husband and two children. Her website is www.jenniferfordberry.com.

DEDICATION

I dedicate this book to everyone in my life whom I call "friend." Your consistent love, support, advice, and laughter are gifts. I consider myself truly blessed for having so many amazing people to share this life with. Thank you!

ACKNOWLEDGMENTS

While writing this book, I spent many hours interviewing experts in business and finance matters. I have learned so much, and I am excited to share this information with you, the reader.

I would like to thank the following people who have contributed their expertise to this book:

Brian Roland, for taking time out of your schedule numerous times to share your valuable insight and experience as a financial advisor with me.

Gigi DeGaine-Roland, for the excellent information you shared with me regarding the human resources field. I cherish your advice and our years of friendship.

Susan Kautz, for giving me the inside scoop on the real estate market. I have been hanging out with you most of my life, and we have yet to share a boring moment!

Lesley Salman, for being one of my most loyal friends and for giving me pointers on selling real estate.

Michelle Pohl: You have really been a blessing to me this year with this book and while we have been building our house. I am glad we have reconnected.

Gary Kriner: How many thank you's do I owe you over the years? More than I can count. Thank you again.

Jessi Boardman: Thank you for proving to me that successful business partnerships do exist. I am so proud of what we have accomplished with Mothertime Marketplace. You are the best partner and a true friend.

Manda Blackwell, for taking time to answer questions and share information for this book.

To Jacqueline Musser: it is a team effort to write these books and I am glad I have you as my editor.

To Suzanne Lucas: my contracts manager, I really appreciate the fact that no matter how busy you are, you always take time to answer my questions and update me on book sales.

Thank you, Dad, for giving me my first business lessons while selling worms and for all of your help this year.

Mom, it takes a special woman to put her own dreams aside to raise three little girls with enough confidence to grow into three women who own their own businesses. Thank you for always supporting my work.

I would like to thank my husband, Josh, for always supporting my business ventures and believing in me, and my children for having patience when Mommy has to work and can't be 100 percent available.

As always, thank you, God, for allowing me to turn my passion for organizing into a career. I feel truly blessed that my job is to write and organize!

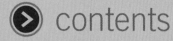 # contents

ORGANIZE YOUR WORK SPACES

ORGANIZE YOUR OWN BUSINESS

ORGANIZE YOUR PERSONAL FINANCES

 # introduction

I wrote this book because starting my own businesses and working for myself has made me a happier person. I want everyone who reads this book to know that if you work hard enough, anything can happen and your dreams will come true!

My dreams of becoming an author, a professional organizer, and running my own business, Mothertime Marketplace, all began with two things: an idea and a belief in myself (one thing money can't buy).

While writing this book, I interviewed and consulted with a number of amazing people who are considered experts in their field so I could present the best practices and most up-to-date information. I have learned so much!

Looking back, it's comical that I had to write about work-life balance because I have been faced with the biggest balancing

challenges of my life while writing this book. I've navigated building a new home and selling my old one. I've increased my work with clients as a professional organizer because all of my children are now in school. I do speaking engagements and book signings.

Everything I do helps me live my dreams. It's exhausting sometimes, but the rewards make up for that! I'm only able to do what I do because I'm organized and intentional with my time and efforts. You can do this, too.

This book will show you how to organize the time and effort you give to your career and finances. It will help you identify your dreams and then create practical steps you can take to make those dreams a reality. Listen to your heart and start your journey.

To follow a deeper call, we must understand that purpose is an inside-out process for: organizing our lives, providing meaning, following our heart and clarifying our calling.

—RICHARD J. LEIDER

THE BASICS OF ORGANIZING
❯ Your Finances & Work Life

How does money affect you and your life?

The recent recession and economic climate have changed our views on careers, personal spending habits, debt, and saving. Many people have experienced feelings of anxiety, stress, and fear due to job loss, foreclosures, or loss of retirement funds. Even though uncertainty is inevitable, we don't have to panic; we can take control of our own personal finances and find ways to actually thrive during economic downturns. Financial security should be more than a wish; it should be your goal and an expectation for your future.

As I mentioned in my first book, *Organize Now! A Week-by-Week Guide to Simplify Your Space and Your Life,* fear is one of the main obstacles preventing people from dealing with their clutter. The same is true for people dealing with their finances. It is completely normal to have fears about your future. The best thing you can do is to first admit and identify your fears. Then you can create plans to ease them and take back control.

Two of the most primary fears people have are the fear of failure and the fear of the future. The fear of failure coincides with our need for significance and purpose. Our fear of the future has to do with our need for security. Money affects both of those needs and can cause much fear and anxiety. We often think, *If I have X amount of money, I will feel secure and important.* We use money and finances to make us feel valuable and important, even though this is not true. Never forget that people are valuable simply because they exist. As the founding fathers of the United States so famously said in the Declaration of Independence, "All men are created equal."

With that being said, we can't just ignore the fact that we *need* money to provide our basic necessities for survival. Personal finances are a reality for everyone, whether you have a net worth of ten thousand dollars or ten million dollars.

About ten years ago I read a book that said the secret to abundance is taking full responsibility for your financial health. When you take responsibility for it, money should stop being a source of frustration and start flowing into your life naturally. At the time, I was very frustrated with my finances and had a hard time believing this to be true. But then I asked myself, *What do I have to lose?* Only good things could come of me being proactive. Today I can honestly say that in my life, this statement has proven to be true. Each time you neglect to handle your finances responsibly, you are sending a message to yourself that you are not a good candidate for more money.

The key to handling money well is to remember that money is simply a tool. You use it to obtain the things you want and need in life. And money can and should be managed. This book will help you organize your time, career, and personal finances so you can manage your money well and increase your earning potential. Organization and money go hand in hand:

- Organizing helps you take control of your physical environment. When you organize your financial affairs, you will take control of your money.
- Organizing eliminates unwanted and unproductive things from your life. When you focus your spending habits and your time, you can

be more intentional with your money and therefore pay off debt, retire early, buy a house, or achieve another major financial goal. Increasing your productivity frees you to have more time to enjoy the things you've worked so hard for, or you can use your time to embark on more money-making endeavors.

The Benefits of Organizing

There are so many benefits to organizing your surroundings and your belongings. For starters, the less clutter you have around you, the more energy you'll have. Don't believe me? Find a cluttered space near you right now and stare at it for sixty seconds. After that minute, note the feelings you have. They may include: stress, anxiety, embarrassment, shame, etc. Now tidy that area up, putting everything in its place and removing the trash. Again stare at the space for sixty seconds. I guarantee you will now feel more positive emotions such as joy, relief, accomplishment, peace, or pride.

Getting organized will save you time. How much time do you waste each week searching for items you have misplaced? These items are buried somewhere in the clutter. How often are you not on time because you are not organized? Are you late getting out the door each morning because you waste time looking for your keys, your kids' schoolwork, or your planner? Taking the time to remove things you don't love or use will inevitably save you time when you are looking for the things that you do use or love.

When you have everything in its place and at your fingertips in your work station, you will be able to sit down and get right to work. You'll be more efficient with your time.

You will also feel more peace and joy in your life. Let's face it, things left undone weigh on us. If you are wishing your life was more organized, chances are this is weighing on your mind every day! It is just another thing sitting on your long to-do list. Take a moment to close your eyes and imagine this life:

- Everything you own has a home, meaning you have a specific place for each item. Things are easy to put back after you are finished using them.
- You arrive to every appointment and meeting on time.
- When you walk into your home or office, you feel energized, happy and proud.
- You spend less time rushing around and stressed out and more time feeling peaceful and living in the moment.

Now doesn't that sound like an ideal life to live? Guess what? It can be done. I am not going to lie and say it won't take work and a major commitment, but I can promise you that the rewards of getting organized are well worth it.

Keys to Time Management

Time management is the foundation for having an organized life. If you learn the skills to correctly manage your time, you will be more productive, feel better about yourself, and reach any goal you set for your life. Each person is given the same amount of time each day. The difference between successful people and unsuccessful people is how they use the time they are given!

PLAN YOUR TIME

The biggest key to organizing your time is to *plan* out your time out before it arrives. Use a planner—paper or electronic—to record your appointments and meetings and to schedule time to accomplish all of your tasks for the day. Each morning list everything you need to accomplish that day in your planner. Then decide the best order for accomplishing each task. You'll never be at a loss for what to do next during the day. If you don't finish a task, move it to your list for the next day.

Set aside some time at the end of the week to plan out the upcoming week. Schedule time to complete to-do items, run errands, go to appointments, etc. Also plan down time for yourself and include open time to spend with those you love.

Purchase a planner that you like the look and feel of and that you find easy to carry and use. You will be more likely to use your planner regularly if you like it.

OVERCOME PROCRASTINATION

Procrastination is one of the biggest ways you can jeopardize your time. Remember, you can't finish what you don't start. Some things just need to be done, whether you want to do them or not. If procrastination is a problem for you, change the way you think. Try these techniques:

- Instead of putting something off for as long as possible, finish the task as quickly as possible. You will be rid of it, and you can move on to things that you actually want to do.
- Decide on a reward you will give yourself only *after* you finish the task.
- Identify why you don't want to do the task and then come up with a solution. Is it boring? Find a way to make it fun.
- Don't let fear hold you back. Often we put things off because we are afraid they will take too much time. Give yourself permission to

Productivity is never an accident. It is always the result of a commitment to excellence, intelligent planning, and focused effort.

—PAUL J. MEYER

take as long as you need on a project or activity. We're also often afraid of failure. Give yourself a pep talk and surround yourself with people who will support you no matter what. We often learn more from our failures than our successes. Don't fear failure. Value the experience as much as the outcome.

HANDLING DISTRACTIONS

Distractions can be a huge waste of time, but many times people actually welcome them. Why? Because distractions and interruptions give them an excuse to stop working—especially if they are working on something they really don't enjoy or want to do. Interrupting your work to deal with a distraction is another form of procrastination.

If you want others to respect your time, then you need to set boundaries to show that you respect your own time. Here's how you can limit distractions and interruptions:

- Let voice mail pick up your calls when you are in the middle of an important project or work that needs to be done. Some landline phones in offices offer a "Do Not Disturb" feature which sends calls straight to voice mail without ringing.
- Silence your cell phone.
- Turn off your e-mail notification while you are working on an important project.
- Put up a "Do Not Disturb" sign on the entrance to your office or desk area to deter people from stopping by to chat.
- Work in an area that has a noise level that allows you to focus best.
- At home, keep pets and children out of the room while you work. Find a sitter if need be.

LEARNING WHEN TO SAY NO

If we are really honest with ourselves when we look at our schedules and long to-do lists, we can usually find "time wasters" to which we should have said no. Most people complain they don't have enough time or they have way too much to do. Why don't they cut back on doing so much? Often it's because they can't say no.

What is it about the word *no* that makes people so uncomfortable about using it? After all, it is our time—our life. The main reason we can't say no is because we want to make someone else happy. We also want to be liked. These are natural desires, but when your people-pleasing pursuits take away from living a happy life, you need to find a balance somewhere in the middle. Making others happy doesn't mean you must make yourself miserable.

There may be another reason why you may have a hard time saying no. Maybe deep down your ego screams, "If I want it done the right way, I have to do it myself!" or "I do everything."

The next time you are asked to do something, don't answer right away. Take a day to mull it over and ask yourself if that is how you want to use your time. Will you enjoy it? Will it move you closer to one of your goals or dreams? Do you actually have the time to do it well? Consult your planner and listen to your gut. Then give the answer that makes you happy instead of trying to please the other person.

Live Your Dreams

This book is not only about how to organize your physical surroundings and paperwork at your work and home office, it's also about organizing your time, resources, and efforts to help you set and accomplish goals and dreams for your future. An organized area is important, and an organized mind is equally as important. Often we must organize our surroundings so we can organize our thoughts.

Cancer therapists Carl and Stephanie Simonton give their patients this advice: "You must stop and reassess your priorities and values. You must be willing to be yourself, not what people want you to be because you think that is the only way you can get love. You can no longer be dishonest. You are now at a point where, if you truly want to live, you have to be who you are."

I think we all could use this advice. Live your dreams now. We tend to judge ourselves based on our success and by the standards society has set for us. However, our worth is not based on our accomplishments. Our worth is irrevocable. Why? Because we were born worthy.

Finding worth in accomplishments and income brackets can ruin your work-life balance. A good work ethic is very important. To do things well we must give each task the full time it deserves. But you also must remember that you work to live. You don't live to work.

If you want to find true work-life balance, you need to find passion. If you can make a living doing something you are passionate about, half the battle is won. You will be killing two birds with one stone each day by going to work—you'll make money *and* feel like you are completing your purpose here on earth.

In her book, *The Passion Test*, Janet Bray Attwood says, "Passion is a very personal experience. When you begin to do what you love, what you are truly passionate about, your life will be irresistibly pulled in directions you can't even begin to imagine." I could not agree with this more because I am living proof of this statement.

I decided to pursue my passion for organizing as a career nearly nine years ago after I was laid off from my corporate career. I took a lot of time contemplating what I wanted to do after I lost my job. I had always earned a great income in corporate America, so I felt like that was where I *should* look for work. But I had always had an entrepreneurial spirit inside of me, and I knew deep down that working for myself would be much more motivating and rewarding. Plus my first child had just been born, and working for myself would give me more flexibility to spend time with her.

After much thought, consulting with mentors, and reading various books, I realized that I was most passionate about organizing, but I wasn't sure I would be able to make enough money doing it as a career. I didn't know anyone else who was in this line of work. I came across a book, *Do What You Love, The Money Will Follow,* and, with a hopeful but skeptical attitude, I started reading it. About halfway through the book I decided to put the advice to work. After all, what did I have to lose? I was unemployed! Soon after, I started advertising for my new organizing business and launched my website and a newsletter called *Weekly Organizing Tips.*

The first day that I was actually *paid* for my organizing services (and not just doing it for free for a friend or family member), I knew I was where I was meant to be on this earth. Little did I know that my little newsletter was building a platform for my future writing career, which was another *huge* dream of mine.

Fast forward to the present: I spend each day doing work I love but, more importantly, I know beyond a shadow of a doubt that I am living my purpose. I am doing what I love and the money did follow.

I share this story with you as encouragement. If I can have my dreams come true, so can you. I am not going to say any of this comes easy; it takes endless motivation, hard work, and perseverance. And *never* take no for an answer the first time.

Let me give you some hard knocks advice: Books are fantastic resources of information that can change your life, but only *you* can put that

Never make financial decisions quickly, irrationally, presumably, or ignorantly. Meaning do your research, take your time, and get the facts before you come to a conclusion. Also, be sure to listen to your heart and your gut. If you made the right decision, you should feel peace, not panic.

advice into action and *make* the changes. Trust me, I wish I could wave my magical organizing wand and everything would miraculously be organized for you (I'd make a lot more money with a wand like that).

One of the main keys to success is to be proactive. Don't sit around complaining about your life and hoping for it to change … *do* something to change it. Don't just read the advice in this book. Live it. The information is written in short goals and tips so you know exactly what to do next. It will take time and effort, but it will be worth it.

Ways to Build Wealth

Because you picked up this book, you are interested in managing your money. You want to manage your money to build your wealth. Here's a secret: You can earn a modest income and be wealthy, and you can earn a large income and be broke. If you spend everything you earn, you are not getting richer!

Here are some keys to building your wealth:

1. Set long-term goals.
2. Spend less.
3. Limit your debt.
4. Be your own bank (increase your liquidity).
5. Invest to preserve your wealth.

Most millionaires live below their means, and only a minority of them drive current-model vehicles. They don't buy brand-new vehicles each year. They drive the same car for many years—which shows two keys at work: spending less and limiting debt.

People who become wealthy use their energy, time, and money in ways that enhance their net worth. It takes time *and* money to care for expensive toys and goods. Most wealthy people spend their money and time on planning their financial future, and studying and managing their current investments. Their goal is to make money so they will be financially secure, not to make money so they can spend it.

Expert Advice

This book covers a number of specific topics, and while I'm an expert professional organizer, I'm not an expert human resources manager or an expert financial plannor. That's why I've consulted several experts in their individual fields and included their advice in this book. These experts are:

- Manda Blackwell, financial advisor for H&H Associates
- Nanette Duffey, Professional Daily Money Manager
- Christopher S. George, financial advisor
- Susan Kautz, Realtor
- Gary Kriner, CPA
- Alicia Myers, owner of gatewaytosaving.com
- Michelle Pohl, accountant
- Gigi DeGaine-Roland, PHR, senior human resources generalist
- Brian Roland, financial advisor for more than eighty players, coaches, and scouts for the NFL and MLB
- Lesley Salman, owner of Salman Home Realty

Several of the weeks in this book include tips directly from professional experts in the specific field related to the topic. All of these tips are indicated with this Expert Advice icon.

Organize Your Time

Organize Your Priorities

When you take control of your time and schedule, you are taking control of your life. And, if you manage your time correctly, your daily tasks should lead to you honoring your priorities and meeting your goals. Your priorities should be the foundation of your schedule and what you devote the majority of your time to. Unfortunately, many of us are simply products of our environment. We get pulled in a hundred directions without ever really steering the time wheel ourselves.

This week will help you identify (or confirm) your priorities so you can honor them and devote more of your time to them. Only *you* can choose how you spend the twenty-four hours you are given each day.

✔	**THIS WEEK'S GOALS:**
☐	Take some time to identify the five most important things in your life. Make these general categories. There are no right or wrong answers to this question, but here are some common responses to help you generate ideas: family, friends, career, pets, spirituality, health, hobbies. Write down your answer.
☐	Create a vision for your life by asking yourself some reflective questions. Give some serious thought to your answers and be sure to write them down. • If you could do or be anything, what would it be? • Where would you live? • What would you do to earn an income? • What would your days be like? • What would you do *more* of? • What would you do *less* of?

Thought becomes intention, this intention has power, and when you put this intention out into the world, your life starts to change—sometimes dramatically.

—CHERYL RICHARDSON

☐ One at a time, evaluate each item you identified and come up with a list of specific goals related to that priority. These goals should be things that you want to do and that help you honor your priorities. Focus on quality, not quantity. Again, there are no right or wrong answers. Here are some examples: Spend more time together by eating dinner together or having a weekly movie or game night, attend my child's sporting activities, get eight hours of sleep each night, exercise three times a week, complete a certification that could lead to a promotion or pay increase, attend a weekly religious service, spend time meditating. Write down these goals.

☐ Evaluate your goals and work them into your schedule. Identify things you can eliminate in order to make more time for your goals. Intention is a very powerful tool. See yourself as meeting your goals. See yourself as living the life you dream of. Tell yourself positive affirmations and negate all negative chatter from your mind and your life.

☐ Break down long-term goals or large, overwhelming goals into steps. Keep breaking them down until you identify a step that you can take right away. Set a timetable for reaching this goal.

☐ Create a special place just for you where you can regularly reflect on your priorities and how you are spending your time. It could be a small nook in your home or a bench next to your favorite garden outside. The size and location doesn't matter. What is important is that you have somewhere to go when you need to check in with yourself.

TIPS:

- Post a written list of your priorities and goals in a place where you can see them and read them each day.

- "Me time" is essential to being a happy, well-rounded person. Most people think they are too busy for personal time. They couldn't possibly take a break because there is just way too much to do! In reality, the opposite is true. If you take some time for yourself, you will actually get more done. You will be more productive and less stressed because you are meeting your own personal needs.

- It takes twenty-one days (or times) to create a new habit. If you are trying to establish a new routine such as a regular exercise or meditation, give yourself enough time to establish the habit before you make changes or give up out of frustration.

NOTES:

Once a Month

☐ Schedule "me time" this month so you can check in with yourself and evaluate if you like how you are spending your time and working toward your goals.

Every 3–6 Months

☐ Take the time to organize and spruce up your special place.

☐ Read an uplifting book that will help you become a better version of yourself in one way or another.

Once a Year

☐ Reflect on all you've accomplished in the past year. Celebrate your successes. Identify things you want to improve in the coming year.

☐ Reevaluate your list of priorities and goals. Identify the five most important things in your life at the moment. Have they changed? If so, set new goals.

Organize Your Five-Year Plan

A five-year plan can be an intimidating thing. Life changes so quickly. How can you possibly know what will happen five years from now? You can't, but you can take steps each day to guide the direction of your life so that at the end of five years, you have reached, or are closer to reaching, your dreams.

When you take time to think about what you want your future to look like, you can devise a plan to make that future a reality. Looking ahead gives you purpose, and having purpose means you know who you are, where you came from, and where you are going. Purpose helps shape our life and keeps us on the right track.

This week is all about dreaming big. Think about what you want for your future. Be willing to open up to the possibilities of what you can be. Do not place limitations on yourself! If you can dream it, you can do it. It may not be easy, but if you make a plan and stick to it, your hard work will take you where you want to go.

✔ THIS WEEK'S GOALS:

☐ Take some time to identify goals and changes you would like to make in the next five years in every aspect of your life. To make this more manageable and focus your thinking, break your life down into these categories and focus on one category at a time, taking frequent breaks or tackling one category per day.

- **Career:** Are you happy in your job? Do you want to work toward a promotion? Would you like to work in a different industry?
- **Family Life:** Are you happy with your relationship status? Will you be starting a family? Will your children be leaving your home to start their own lives?

One purpose in life is not more important than another. There is purpose whenever we use our gifts and talents to respond to something we believe in.

—*RICHARD J. LEIDER*

- **Social Life:** Are you happy with the number of friends you have? Do you participate in clubs or other organizations where you can interact with others and meet new people?
- **Living Situation:** Would you like to buy a house or pay off your house? Will you downsize to a smaller home or move to a different city?
- **Financial Situation:** Do you want to be debt free? How can you spend less or increase your income?

☐ Working on one goal at a time, identify everything you will need to do to reach each that goal. Make a list and then use this list to create a step-by-step plan. If a step seems too big or overwhelming, break it down into smaller steps until you feel as if you can manage it.

☐ Set deadlines for when you will complete each step in your plan. Be realistic in your timing. Give yourself enough time to complete a task, but don't leave the deadline so vague or distant that you never get around to it. This is a five-year plan, so don't expect to get everything done in six months. It may be helpful to identify milestones you would like to accomplish each year, on your way to achieving your ultimate goal, so you can measure your progress and not get overwhelmed by the entire goal.

☐ Share your goals with people you trust. This will make you more accountable, and, hopefully, these people will help support you. You don't have to share every goal with one person, although you may choose to share them all with your spouse so you are on the same page. When seeking outside support, be selective. Share career goals with a mentor. Share social goals with a close friend. Share financial goals with your financial advisor.

☐ Start a "My Goals" notebook. Write down every single desire you have, no matter how big or small. Carry it with you so you can capture new goals when they occur to you. Act on short-term goals immediately. Take time to set up workable plans for long-term goals. Writing out your goals sends a powerful message to your subconscious.

 TIPS:

- Consider taking personality tests, skills tests, or aptitude tests to help you find a career you can be passionate about.

- A career mentor or coach can help you identify steps you need to take to carry out your five-year plan at work.

- Make sure the goals you set are worthwhile and important enough for you to desire to work hard to reach them.

- You must be willing to work to achieve your goals. Simply listing your goals won't accomplish them.

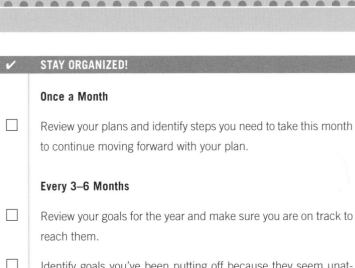

STAY ORGANIZED!

Once a Month

☐ Review your plans and identify steps you need to take this month to continue moving forward with your plan.

Every 3–6 Months

☐ Review your goals for the year and make sure you are on track to reach them.

☐ Identify goals you've been putting off because they seem unattainable. Seek advice from someone who has accomplished a similar goal and put a plan in place.

Once a Year

☐ Reflect on everything you accomplished in the previous year. Celebrate your victories.

☐ Set clear goals for the year and create monthly plans for achieving them.

☐ Review your five-year plan. Is it still what you want? Make adjustments based on how you've grown and changed in the past year.

NOTES:

_____

_____

_____

_____

_____

Organize Your Time Management Skills

I guarantee that 90 percent of you who read this book feel like you have too much to do. We all have things to do; what separates those who are efficient and successful with their time from those who are not is the *way* they do things. In other words, it's the way we manage our time.

✔ THIS WEEK'S GOALS:

☐ Keep a time log for one week. Map out your day in increments of thirty minutes and write down what you do during each half hour. Carry this log with you so you can update it accurately. It will take less than a minute each hour if you keep up with it. Include any unplanned distractions such as socializing with a co-worker or zoning out on the Internet. Be honest. You are the only person who will see this.

☐ Evaluate your time log from the previous week and look for time-wasters. You will probably be surprised at how much time you frittered away. You can change your habits only when you are aware of them. Be intentional about eliminating time-wasters from your days.

☐ Be realistic about how much you can accomplish. People struggle with time management for two reasons: Either they try to do too much, or they have too much time, so they never get started. Your time log will give you a good idea of how long it takes you to complete tasks. Don't take on more than you can handle.

☐ Be more selective with how you spend your time. The next time someone asks you to spend your time doing something, no matter what it is, look at your schedule to see if you have time, and then

Our most valuable asset is time, and successful achievers spend this precious commodity more carefully than money.

—ZIG ZIGLAR

check your priority list and ask yourself if that is how you want to spend your time.

☐ Make it a habit to focus on one thing at a time. I love to multi-task just as much as the next person, but sometimes this can be a real time-waster. You may feel more productive when you juggle more than one task at a time, but it's only when these tasks are completed that you can really cross them off your list. Concentrate on completion instead of juggling. You can still work on multiple projects throughout the day. Simply work on each project one at a time. If you can't finish something, decide on a good stopping point and then move on to your next task when you reach it.

☐ Eliminate interruptions and distractions while you are working on a project. Turn off your e-mail notification and check your e-mail once an hour, or once in the morning and once in the afternoon. Screen your phone calls and check your voice mail at set times when you can return calls.

☐ Work on being specific and clear in your requests. Being vague about what you need or want might save you time now, but it will cost you a lot more time in the future when you have to reexplain yourself or when misunderstandings lead to mistakes. Take a few extra minutes the first time to be precise with what you are communicating.

☐ When someone asks you for something ASAP, ask for a specific deadline so you can accurately prioritize that task.

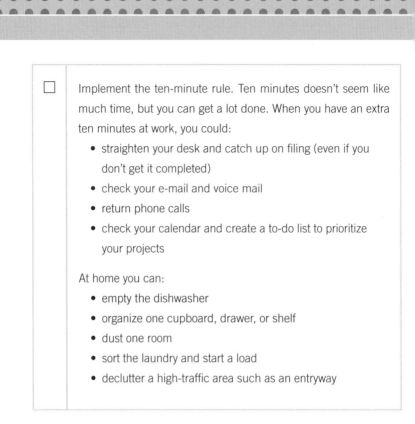

Implement the ten-minute rule. Ten minutes doesn't seem like much time, but you can get a lot done. When you have an extra ten minutes at work, you could:

- straighten your desk and catch up on filing (even if you don't get it completed)
- check your e-mail and voice mail
- return phone calls
- check your calendar and create a to-do list to prioritize your projects

At home you can:

- empty the dishwasher
- organize one cupboard, drawer, or shelf
- dust one room
- sort the laundry and start a load
- declutter a high-traffic area such as an entryway

 TIPS:

- Studies have shown that successful people do one thing at a time. They are able to concentrate better, complete the task in less time, and make fewer errors.

- Remember the 80/20 rule: 20 percent of your activities will account for 80 percent of your effectiveness. Devote the most time and energy to activities that make you effective.

- Always carry a day planner with you. It can be paper or electronic. Consult your calendar before you set any appointment.

- Consult your calendar every night so you know what to expect for the next day.

- Aim to accomplish only three major tasks each day. This will help you focus on your work and achieve your goal, which will keep you motivated. If you take on too much, you may not accomplish anything.

✔	**STAY ORGANIZED!**

Once a Month

☐ Identify a task you would like to do more efficiently. Brainstorm ways you could do it faster. Ask other people how they handle the task and try their ideas.

☐ Evaluate your schedule for the month and eliminate some items if you have taken on too much.

Every 3–6 Months

☐ Keep another time log and compare it to previous logs. How have you improved your time management skills? What could be improved?

Once a Year

☐ Buy a new planner or calendar.

NOTES:

_____

_____

_____

_____

_____

Organize Your Work-Life Balance

We are a work-centered culture! We have been conditioned to think that work should bring us fulfillment, give us our identity, measure our value, and improve our lives. This is not true. You've heard the mantra, *work to live, don't live to work*. Now's the time to put this into practice. Remember, "No" is a complete sentence. The reason why it is hard to say no is because we are worried about what the other person will think of us. We make our own choices, and it is only up to us how we spend our time.

✔	THIS WEEK'S GOALS:

☐ Evaluate your work week. How many hours are you working each day? How many hours are you expected to work each day? If you are salaried, talk to your human resources representative to confirm how many hours you are expected to work each day and each week. How many hours do you want to work each day?

☐ Establish how many overtime hours you are willing to work on a regular basis. Sure, there are days when you just have to stay late and finish the job, but this shouldn't happen every day. You don't need to communicate this to your supervisor. Use this limit to help you decide if you want to pick up an extra shift or voluntary overtime when it is offered.

☐ If you work from home or are self-employed, set regular office hours and stick to them. Schedule a start time, a morning break, lunch time, an afternoon break, and an end time for each day. If possible, use the same schedule every day, or for as many days a week as possible. Let your family know these hours. Stick with this schedule for at least a month. It takes twenty-one days to

Stop feeling pressured to lead a perfectly balanced life ... Don't feel guilty that some aspect of your life is getting short shrift. If you do the best you can, it will be more than enough.

—SYLVIE ROCHETTE

create a new habit, so give it time to take effect. Keep your work in an office and separate from the rest of your home.

☐ Identify one or two personal activities (attend your child's soccer game or go to the gym) you would like to do after work each week, and make it a priority to leave work early enough to accomplish these.

☐ Make it a goal to have some amount of free time each day. Free time is not twenty minutes left over at the end of the day a couple times a week. It is something you should make time for in your schedule every day.

☐ Create a support network at work so your co-workers can help cover for you when you need help.

☐ Plan meals once a week, before you go to the grocery store. You can buy all the ingredients you need, and you will always know what to make for dinner when you get home from work. Plus, things will be defrosted, or you can use a slow cooker to cook dinner while you are at work. This saves you a lot of time and stress and helps you feed yourself and your family well.

☐ Set a firm bedtime for yourself during the work week. Begin to wind down from your day at least forty-five minutes before your set bedtime. When wind-down time starts, shut off your computer and turn off your e-mail/message notification on your phone. Don't accept work phone calls after this time. If you have a hard time shutting down, keep a piece of paper with you and make a list of things to do the next day (not right now). You will free your mind from the worry of forgetting.

☐ Use one of your weekend days as a day off from work and from chores. Give yourself a full day of rest at least once a week. To do this, you will need to prioritize your chores and errands throughout the week or on your other day off, but it will be worth it.

☐ Distribute household responsibilities among family members. Create a chore chart to help. Set minimum standards for what needs to be accomplished. As long as these are met, don't worry if things aren't done exactly as you would have done them.

 TIPS:

- Work on saying no when someone asks you to do something that is not on your priority list.

- Establish boundaries with others when necessary.

- Before you leave work, reach a good stopping point for the project you are working on so you can start fresh the next day and not worry about it at home.

- If possible, commute with your spouse for some extra one-on-one time.

- If grandparents or other family members are willing to help out with your children, let them! It will help lighten your load and build bonds between your children and their relatives.

Once a Month

☐ Plan a special day just for yourself and your family or friends to spend time together. Be creative; it doesn't need to cost money. Put it on your schedule so you are firmly committed to it.

☐ If you eat out for lunch during your workday, multitask and meet a friend occasionally.

Every 3–6 Months

☐ Evaluate how many hours you spend working compared to how much time you spend on your personal life. Make changes if needed.

Once a Year

☐ As you set your yearly goals at work, be sure they allow you to live a full life outside of work. Decide if working toward a promotion will be worth the personal sacrifices you will need to make.

NOTES:

_____

_____

_____

_____

_____

_____

_____

_____

Organize Your Day Planner

There is one organizing principle I have said a *million* times: "Everything needs a home." This principle applies to time as well. You can't bottle time, but you can record it. It is the recording of your time that needs a home. The best home for your time record is a day planner. A day planner gives you one central location to track and store all of your to-dos, appointments, phone calls, and reminders. Using a day planner should eliminate all the little scraps of paper that are scattered all over your desk, office, and countertops (including the ones buried in your purse, pockets, or briefcase). Keeping all of this information in *one* day planner will save time and reduce stress.

It is important to use a planner that is specific to your needs; after all, this will be the *one* place where you will store your schedule and to-dos. It should be portable enough to take with you anywhere, durable, secure, and you should absolutely love the look and feel of it. If don't like it, you won't use it! There should be ample room for appointments, phone calls, errands, to-dos and an integrated calendar that works for your weekly and monthly schedule.

✔ THIS WEEK'S GOALS:

☐ Use only one day planner. It will contain both your work and personal schedule. Using more than one planner will leave room for overlapped activities and missed appointments. If you have a planner but don't use it, ask yourself why you don't use it. You probably don't like it. Give yourself permission to buy a new one that you will be excited about using. As you look for a new planner, ask yourself these questions to help you find a planner that will meet your needs:

- Do you prefer to write or type? If you write, do you tend to write small or large?

Today is a gift. That's why it is called the present. Open it carefully, use it wisely, and don't forget to say thank you.

—UNKNOWN

- Do you need a calendar that follows the calendar year or the school year?
- How do you best visualize time? Do you want a vertical or horizontal format? Do you want the hours broken down by minutes? Do you want a month-at-a-glance, weekly or daily view? Do you need two or three different views in one planner?
- Will you keep loose papers in this planner? If so, consider one that has folder pockets or zips up to properly contain the extra papers.
- What would be the ideal size of your planner? Do you want it to fit in a bag, purse, or briefcase?

☐ You may find that a PDA or smartphone will fit your needs better than a paper planner. Some advantages to this format are:

- It's easy to create a backup.
- It's easy to read and update. It eliminates crossed out information, eraser marks, and unclear handwriting.

Some potential disadvantages are:

- It's more expensive.
- It's a little more complicated to use and, therefore, there may be a longer learning curve.

☐ Gather your work calendar and your family calendar and any other calendars you use (such as your partner's work-shift calendar). Enter all of the information on each calendar into your planner. From now on, record all activities in your planner first. You can still keep a family calendar so everyone in the home knows what's

41

going on, but update the family calendar after you update your day planner, and include work schedules on the family calendar.

 Collect all of the loose pieces of paper that contain your to-do lists, appointment times, reminders, and invitations. Transfer all of this information into your new planner. You can create different lists for work to-dos and personal to-dos.

TIPS:

- Before you go to a store to purchase a planner, check online to view different planners and find styles you think will work for you. Check out *Organize Now! 12 Month Home & Activity Planner* on the website of your favorite online bookseller. Other sites to explore are www.busybodybook.com, www.dayrunner.com, www.daytimer.com, and www.franklincovey.com.

- Take your planner with you everywhere you go. Leave it in your car if you don't think you'll need it and retrieve it if you find you do.

- Enter information in your planner as soon as possible. Include time, address, and phone number for all activities so you can call if you are running late or look up the address if you get lost.

- Use a planner for at least three months before you decide it is not the right one for you. If you are not currently using a day planner, it may take some discipline to get on the right track with this tool. Like exercise, you may have to force yourself until it becomes habit!

- Always create a backup for your planner. If you use a digital planner, this will be a piece of cake. If you use a paper system, you can simply photocopy essential pages. If you misplace your planner, you'll be thankful you have a backup.

STAY ORGANIZED!

Once a Month

☐ At the beginning of every month, look ahead in your planner so you have a pretty good idea of what your schedule looks like.

☐ Update your family calendar using the information in your day planner.

☐ If you keep loose paper in your planner, sort through the papers and dispose of any outdated information.

Every 3–6 Months

☐ Update the backup for your planner.

Once a Year

☐ Purchase refill pages for your planner or make sure your software is up-to-date if using an electronic device.

☐ Transfer any birthdays and anniversaries to your new planner pages.

NOTES:

Organize Your To-Do List

Things left undone linger in the back of your mind. The need to constantly remember them steals your energy (and your sleep!). A to-do list captures your thoughts and your responsibilities. It helps you plan your time efficiently and frees you from the stress of remembering and the fear of forgetting.

Unfortunately, simply listing all of your responsibilities won't get them done, so this week will also provide you with some ideas about how to accomplish more on your to-do list. It will help you concentrate your efforts so you can devote all of your attention to one task at a time and finish it faster.

As with a day planner, it's important to keep only *one* to-do list for the day. You may, however, find it too distracting to have your personal to-dos mixed in with your work to-dos. If that is the case, separate the list into two columns—work and personal—and tackle each at the appropriate times.

✔ THIS WEEK'S GOALS:

☐ Decide where you would like to keep your to-do list. You can use a simple notepad that lets you jot down tasks when they spring to mind, or you can use a software program on an electronic device. If you keep this list with or in your planner, planning your time will be even more effective and efficient because you can quickly plan around any appointments and schedule time to run errands and make phone calls.

☐ Create a master to-do list that includes everything you need to accomplish in at least the next month; add tasks further in the future if you already are aware of them. You will add to this list in the future as needed. Place deadlines next to the tasks if they need to be completed by a specific date. This is a rough draft. Don't worry about listing things in order.

The typical office worker only spends half of the time on A and B priorities. But top performers spend 60 percent or more of their time on As and Bs. So the difference between average and great performance is just one extra hour per day spent on the things that really count.

—MARK ELLWOOD

☐ Now go through your master list and assign each item a letter according to time sensitivity:

A—Needs to be completed today or this week

B—Needs to be completed this month

C—You want to complete it when you have some extra time

The main difference between an A task and a B task is that an A task is your first priority and a B task still has a deadline but in the somewhat distant future.

☐ Schedule time in your planner right now for your A tasks. Be realistic and plan to accomplish just three tasks each day. If you finish them and have more time, you have a choice to continue working on A tasks or focusing on B, or even C, tasks.

☐ If you are using software, rearrange your master list so all the Bs are together, followed by all the Cs. Place them in order of time sensitivity within the two letter groups. If you are writing by hand, do the same on a fresh piece of paper, and then discard the original, unorganized list.

☐ Use your master to-do list and day planner to plan your schedule each week. Again, be realistic about what you can accomplish. Aim for three things so you feel successful and don't get overwhelmed. If an A task pops up during the day, add it to the end of your list for the day. What you don't accomplish today can be put on tomorrow's to-do list or scheduled for later in the week. The most important thing is to record new tasks on your list and not on random pieces of paper.

 TIPS:

- Be clear about what you want to accomplish in a designated time frame.

- Keep your time balanced. Do not overwork in one area so that you end up neglecting another area.

- If you have a lot going on, you can divide your to-do list by category.

- Accept the reality that you usually will not get every single item on your list done every single day. Tomorrow is a new day, so give yourself permission to let it go.

- Beware of extreme perfectionism. Remember, only God is perfect! Be happy just doing your best.

NOTES:

STAY ORGANIZED!

Once a Month

☐ At the beginning of each month, start scheduling your B tasks in your planner.

☐ Glance at your C tasks so you will know what you should be working on if you find some extra time. Move some C tasks to B tasks if they've been hanging around on your list for a long time. If you want to accomplish something, you need to make time instead of waiting for free time.

Every 3–6 Months

☐ Make it a goal to complete a minimum of three C tasks on your list.

Once a Year

☐ Reflect on what you wanted to accomplish in the previous year and what you actually accomplished. Brainstorm ideas for the upcoming year that will help you meet your goals.

☐ Consider starting a fresh notebook of to-dos for the upcoming year.

Organize Your Workday

Whether you like to admit it or not, being unorganized at work *does* affect your productivity. Experts estimate that people waste thirty minutes to one hour *per day* searching for something they need but can't find at work. This adds up to five hours per week of lost time!

There are a few keys to having a productive workday. Start by prioritizing tasks each day. Establish routines and schedules to efficiently complete reoccurring tasks. Be strategic about meetings, and have an agenda to make the best use of time and keep everyone on the same page. Have a plan for managing phone calls and e-mails. The average person wastes thirty minutes per day searching through e-mails. The goals and tips for this week will help you keep your workday manageable and productive.

✔	THIS WEEK'S GOALS:
☐	Make the first hour of your day really count. What is the one thing that you never have enough time for? Start a new habit of doing this task when you first arrive at work. If you find you spend much of the first hour at the office chatting and gossiping with co-workers, set a break time for later in the morning to catch up or eat lunch together.
☐	Start each workday with a realistic plan. Identify the most important tasks for the day and dedicate time to completing, or making significant progress, on each one.
☐	Batch like activities and tasks together. Visit the mail room only once per day. Try to make all of your photocopies at the same time. Try to make most of your outgoing calls one right after the other. A dedicated phone time (be it ten minutes or an hour)

Hard work is often the easy work you did not do at the proper time.

—BERNARD MELTZER

will leave your phone line open for the remainder of the day so people can contact you if needed. You'll also be available when people stop by your desk.

☐ Use the last twenty to thirty minutes of your day to organize and prepare for the following day. Identify your priorities for the next day, and then check your calendar for meetings and schedule your work around them. It's a good way to wind down the workday, when you may be mentally tired. It will also let you jump right into work when you arrive the next morning.

☐ Slow down. Trying to work as fast as you possibly can leaves too much room for mistakes and adds to your stress.

☐ Underpromise and overdeliver. If you think you can deliver a request within four hours, tell them the end of the day. They will be thrilled when you deliver early. You will be covered in case an urgent request demands your time and takes you away from the task or you find the task is more time-intensive than you expected. You'll also have time to double-check your work.

☐ Before you schedule a meeting, evaluate whether a meeting is the most effective way to communicate and accomplish what needs to be done. Sometimes it's more productive to have a conference call or send an e-mail.

☐ Limit the number of times you check your e-mail during the day. For example, check your e-mail at the top of every hour, or less if you can get away with it. A rule of thumb is to check your e-mail before you need to scroll down from the top to view additional new messages. Turn off your e-mail notification sound, especially when you are trying to get work done. That noise is an automatic interruption that you can eliminate right now.

☐ Set your e-mail account on preview mode so you can read the first few lines of an e-mail and assess its urgency without opening it all the way.

☐ Set up folders within your Inbox to help you keep your e-mails organized. Include folders titled "To Do" or "To Reply" for those e-mails that require your attention but that you currently cannot address.

☐ Set up your signature option so that all e-mails you send have your accurate contact information.

☐ Keep your Inbox empty by deleting unneeded e-mails and immediately moving e-mails to a more appropriate folder (such as, "To Do," "To Reply," or a specific project folder if it's general information you will need to reference again).

TIPS:

- When trying to decide which task to tackle next, ask yourself these questions: How much time do I have available right now? What is the highest prioritized task I can fit into this time frame?

- A person is much more likely to attend one of your meetings again if you end on time or a little early.

- Delete all spam without opening it. If you open it, the sender will know they have a "live" e-mail address. Don't forget to mark new spam so it stops appearing in your Inbox.

- If you are not sure how someone will interpret the tone of your e-mail or text message, call the person instead.

- Always write a concise, specific description in the subject line of any e-mail you send.

- Use the tools available with your e-mail software to apply rules, block senders, color code new messages, apply labels, and more.

- Place the most important part of your e-mail in the first three lines. Include what you want or need. Many people use the preview setting on their e-mail to decide which e-mails to open. If the content is time-sensitive, put the deadline in the subject line also.

- The average employee loses thirty-one hours a month in unproductive meetings. The average person's attention span is sixty to ninety minutes. If your meeting must go longer than this, schedule breaks.

- When you are out of the office, turn on the out-of-office auto response for your e-mail. Include the dates you will be out and the date you will return in the auto-response message. Change your voice mail message to list the dates you are out and when you will return. Your contacts will know when to follow up with you and that you are not ignoring their correspondence.

- When writing an e-mail, use bullets points instead of a paragraph format when there are multiple things you need or want.

- When you leave a voice mail for someone, speak slowly and include your name, the reason for your call, and the best time to reach you, and state your phone number twice.

NOTES:

_____

_____

_____

_____

_____

_____

_____

_____

_____

_____

_____

_____

_____

_____

_____

_____

_____

_____

_____

_____

Once a Month

☐ Change your voice mail greeting.

☐ Take a close look at the month ahead. Note important deadlines and make a specific schedule for meeting them.

☐ Clean up your e-mail. Remove e-mails from your "To-Do" folder that have been completed. Empty your Spam.

Every 3–6 Months

☐ Take a closer look at your workday and consider ways that you can make better use of your time. Implement these changes.

☐ Evaluate the effectiveness of any weekly meetings you attend. Are the meetings still serving a purpose? Do you need to continue having these meetings?

☐ Evaluate any productivity goals you set at the beginning of the year? Have you met these goals, or are you on track to do so?

☐ Make sure your contact lists are updated to save time in the future.

Once a Year

☐ Set productivity goals for the coming year. Be realistic, but also give yourself something to aspire to. For example, you could try to find a more efficient way to complete a routine task or aim to schedule fewer meetings or decrease the length of the meetings you attend.

☐ Go through your e-mail Inbox folders to make sure the titles are still accurate. Delete any folders that you no longer use.

Organize Your Meetings & Appointments

The average employee loses thirty-one hours a month in unproductive meetings—that's nearly four full working days! So it's no wonder so many people dread attending yet another meeting in the middle of their workdays. But a well-organized meeting can energize people by generating great ideas, solving problems, and helping employees work more efficiently by identifying goals and action items.

This week we'll look at ways to make your meetings as efficient and productive as possible. I'll also give you strategies for when to schedule meetings and tips for making it to appointments on time.

✔ **THIS WEEK'S GOALS:**

☐ Before you schedule a meeting, identify what you want to accomplish during the meeting, and then consider if this can be accomplished only in a meeting or if it can be accomplished outside of a meeting.

☐ Identify tasks people can do before the meeting to make the meeting more productive and efficient. For example, if you are having a creative/brainstorming meeting, ask participants to come to the meeting with five ideas written down so you have a place to start the discussion and everyone has something to contribute.

☐ Create a specific agenda for every meeting you set, and stick to the agenda. Discuss the most important issues of the meeting first and the least important issues at the end. You'll have people's full attention in the beginning, and you can end the meeting on time even if you don't get to every item on the agenda. Type up the agenda and send it out to attendees at least

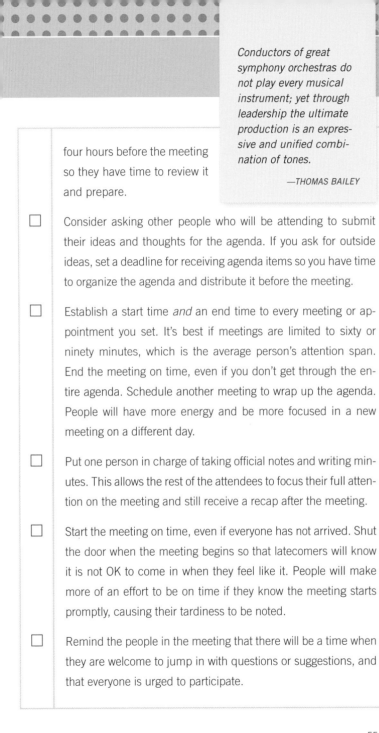

four hours before the meeting so they have time to review it and prepare.

> *Conductors of great symphony orchestras do not play every musical instrument; yet through leadership the ultimate production is an expressive and unified combination of tones.*
>
> —THOMAS BAILEY

☐ Consider asking other people who will be attending to submit their ideas and thoughts for the agenda. If you ask for outside ideas, set a deadline for receiving agenda items so you have time to organize the agenda and distribute it before the meeting.

☐ Establish a start time *and* an end time to every meeting or appointment you set. It's best if meetings are limited to sixty or ninety minutes, which is the average person's attention span. End the meeting on time, even if you don't get through the entire agenda. Schedule another meeting to wrap up the agenda. People will have more energy and be more focused in a new meeting on a different day.

☐ Put one person in charge of taking official notes and writing minutes. This allows the rest of the attendees to focus their full attention on the meeting and still receive a recap after the meeting.

☐ Start the meeting on time, even if everyone has not arrived. Shut the door when the meeting begins so that latecomers will know it is not OK to come in when they feel like it. People will make more of an effort to be on time if they know the meeting starts promptly, causing their tardiness to be noted.

☐ Remind the people in the meeting that there will be a time when they are welcome to jump in with questions or suggestions, and that everyone is urged to participate.

When a new issue that is not part of the agenda comes up, table the discussion and write the issue at the bottom of your agenda. If you have time, cover it at the end of the meeting, or add these items to the agenda for your next meeting.

 TIPS:

- If e-mails are going back and forth, it may be time to schedule a meeting face-to-face to save time.

- Send out the agenda ahead of time so the people attending can be prepared.

- Always turn off your electronic devices when you enter a meeting or appointment.

- If you are hosting a meeting, send out a reminder e-mail or text message thirty minutes prior to starting.

- Mondays are the worst day to schedule a meeting.

- If you are invited to a meeting that doesn't include an end time, ask the meeting's organizer how long the meeting is expected to last. Note the end time in your calendar so you know how much time to block off for the meeting.

- If a meeting is running long, excuse yourself so you do not miss your next commitment.

- Always arrive on time to a meeting. Don't wait until the start time to leave your desk.

- Always thank everyone for attending at the end of a meeting.

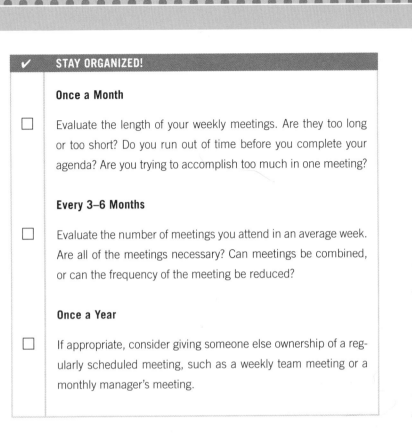

STAY ORGANIZED!

Once a Month

☐ Evaluate the length of your weekly meetings. Are they too long or too short? Do you run out of time before you complete your agenda? Are you trying to accomplish too much in one meeting?

Every 3–6 Months

☐ Evaluate the number of meetings you attend in an average week. Are all of the meetings necessary? Can meetings be combined, or can the frequency of the meeting be reduced?

Once a Year

☐ If appropriate, consider giving someone else ownership of a regularly scheduled meeting, such as a weekly team meeting or a monthly manager's meeting.

NOTES:

Organize Your E-mail

The biggest mistake most people make with their e-mail is letting their Inboxes be catchalls for every e-mail they receive. Think of your Inbox the same way think of your physical mailbox. If you never took the mail out of that box, it would soon be way too cluttered to use, and It would take way too long to sort through everything in it. Your Inbox should only be used to deliver the e-mail to you. After you open an e-mail, place it in another clearly labeled folder or delete it.

✔ THIS WEEK'S GOALS:

☐ Consolidate all personal e-mails into one account. Having more than one account is too time-consuming and increases your chance of missing a message.

☐ Set up folders in your e-mail for each type of message you receive, just like you do in a physical filing cabinet. Categories could include coupons, pictures, banking, and project-specific folders. Make them as specific as you can so e-mails can easily be retrieved when you need them.

☐ Create an "Action" folder or "To Do" folder to contain e-mails that require an action from you. Flag them for follow-up and set a reminder note on the flag so you don't forget.

☐ Sort incoming mail by subject, keyword, or author so you can process related e-mails together.

☐ Block off times to check and process your e-mail, and stick to that time frame. We have all been victims of wasting too much time reading and handling e-mail. Turn off your e-mail notification if you're too distracted or tempted by it.

> *It is easier to act yourself into a better way of feeling than to feel yourself into a better way of action.*
>
> —O.H. MOWRER

☐ Don't waste your time with un-wanted promotional e-mails from businesses. Unsubscribe from e-mail lists if you never read the company's e-mails or click "report spam" so future messages go to your junk folder. Be selective in giving out your e-mail address. If you must provide an e-mail address, look for a box that will let you opt out of receiving marketing e-mails.

☐ Take the time to set up an accurate, efficient address book to save contact information. Sort addresses into groups or lists when needed.

☐ Set your e-mail to preview mode so you won't have to open the e-mail all the way to see whether you want to read it.

☐ Review the settings on your antivirus and spam software to be sure they are adequately blocking all unwanted e-mail.

NOTES:

_____

_____

_____

_____

_____

_____

_____

_____

_____

TIPS:

- Always use the spell-check option before sending an e-mail.

- Carefully consider what you write. Your message will remain on servers even after it has been deleted by the recipient. E-mails can also be easily forwarded to others.

- Use descriptive subject lines to raise your chance of having the e-mail read. People receive many e-mails each day, and often only skim subject lines to see what is interesting or urgent.

- Use autoresponders to send frequently requested information. This will save time and be professional.

- After you have saved a received document onto your hard drive, delete the e-mail. These docs take up a lot of space on the server.

- Use the BCC feature when necessary, and be careful about using Reply All when responding to a message. Always use the BCC feature on your own e-mail lists and announcements to protect the privacy of the recipients.

- Always double-check the e-mail address you are sending your message to before you hit send so you can verify the message is going to the intended recipient.

- Be careful with punctuation. You can imply the wrong message by overusing question marks and exclamation points.

- As with regular paper, the 80/20 rule also applies to e-mail. You will reread only 20 percent of the e-mails you save. The other 80 percent will end up cluttering up your folders. Make a decision *now* whether you need to save this e-mail, and delete items you don't need.

- If you do not have time to answer an e-mail immediately, click Reply and then save it to your Draft box so you are reminded to respond when you have time.

✔	STAY ORGANIZED!

Once a Month

☐ Update your contact list when you receive an e-mail from someone you will need to contact in the future.

☐ Go through old e-mails and reply or delete them.

Every 3–6 Months

☐ Go through each folder in your e-mail and remove all unnecessary e-mails. Old messages congest servers and slow them down.

☐ Clean out your Sent, Trash, and Spam boxes.

Once a Year

☐ Register or purchase any antivirus or spam detector software you use.

Organize Long-Term Projects

It's easy to let a long-term project slide, especially if the due date is months away. Whether you are intentionally putting off the project or simply lulled by the thought that you have plenty of time, procrastination is the biggest obstacle to completion.

Procrastination doesn't remove our responsibility for completing the project. It just delays the inevitable and adds unnecessary stress. Why not just get this task over with and move on?

The key to organizing a long-term project is to create a simple plan that will realistically work with both your experience and the time you have available. Proper planning in the beginning will ensure the project is completed accurately and on time. It is also best to work on the project during the time of day when you are most motivated and energized.

✔ THIS WEEK'S GOALS:

☐ Gather all the requirements, facts, expectations, and due dates concerning the project before you begin. Ask questions if things aren't clear. If you need specific information, keep asking for it until you receive it.

☐ Clearly define the objective of your project. Picture the end result in your mind. Post this definition so you (and maybe the group you are working with) will see it at all times. This will constantly remind you of the reason for your hard work and hopefully keep you motivated as well.

☐ Contact anyone else assigned to this project, or contact people who you would like to help. Coordinate schedules and plan meeting times now for the duration of the project.

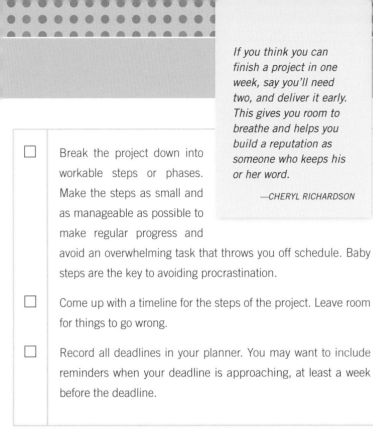

> *If you think you can finish a project in one week, say you'll need two, and deliver it early. This gives you room to breathe and helps you build a reputation as someone who keeps his or her word.*
>
> —CHERYL RICHARDSON

☐ Break the project down into workable steps or phases. Make the steps as small and as manageable as possible to make regular progress and avoid an overwhelming task that throws you off schedule. Baby steps are the key to avoiding procrastination.

☐ Come up with a timeline for the steps of the project. Leave room for things to go wrong.

☐ Record all deadlines in your planner. You may want to include reminders when your deadline is approaching, at least a week before the deadline.

 TIPS:

- The average month contains twenty-two workdays. Use this as a starting point when you map out the deadlines for your project. Try to do some work each day on this project.

- It is better to do one small thing than nothing at all!

- Ask someone you trust to make sure you are accountable and on the right track to complete the project. Give this person a copy of your timeline so he can check in with you on specific dates.

- Reward yourself for each deadline you meet. Don't forget to check off each step you complete—this is very rewarding!

STAY ORGANIZED!

Once a Month

☐ Update your timeline and include any additional steps that you have realized need to be covered before the project is complete.

☐ Credit anyone else who has worked on a project with you.

Every 3–6 Months

☐ Review the steps you have already completed and pat yourself on the back for a job well done.

Once a Year

☐ Look ahead and think about long-term projects that you would like to complete in the upcoming year. Write them down with your C tasks.

NOTES:

_____

_____

_____

_____

_____

_____

_____

_____

_____

Organize Your Career

Organize Your Career Goals

It is crucial that you check in with yourself on a regular basis about your personal goals and dreams. This is your life, not someone else's, so live it the way you want to. Many times people do what others want them to do instead of following their own heart. Or they let fear hold them back. The fear of failure is very powerful. Is this fear affecting your decision making? Worry is an attempt to control the future. This week will help you identify your career goals and create a plan so you can reach those goals.

✔ THIS WEEK'S GOALS:

☐ Write a list of all the things that define success for you. Happiness? Paying your bills on time? Respect? Raising awareness? Increasing productivity in someone's life? There are no right or wrong answers.

☐ Write down what you would like to accomplish with your career. Next to each goal write down when you would like to meet it.

☐ Honestly assess your skills and interests. Ask yourself:
- What am I passionate about?
- What do I have experience with?
- What are my strengths?
- What are my weaknesses?

☐ Ask yourself: If I could do anything, what would I do? What would my work environment look like and how would it feel? How flexible do I want my career to be? How many hours would I like to work? How far am I willing to go from my current home to find work?

> *When you follow your bliss ... doors will open where you would not have thought there would be doors; and where there wouldn't be a door for anyone else.*
>
> —JOSEPH CAMPBELL

☐ Take one or more career assessment tests. These tests should be one of your first steps in researching careers if you are unsure about the right path to take.

☐ Consider volunteering in the field you're interested in.

☐ Attend a job or career fair.

☐ Arrange a job shadow.

☐ Do your research. Learn everything you can about the type of career you want to pursue. Gather the following information and compare it to what you've learned about yourself in the previous goals:

- How much education/training will you need?
- How much will this education cost?
- What is the average annual income?
- What's the demand for this job?
- How crowded and competitive is the job market for this position?
- Where is this job available?

Find the answers to these questions and receive online career counseling at www.careers.org. The Bureau of Labor Statistics' Occupational Outlook Handbook, available at www.bls.gov/oco, will tell you what education and training is required, employment prospects for hundreds of different careers.

- [ ] Use the SWOT method: Analyze your own Strengths, Weaknesses, Opportunities, and Threats.

- [ ] Schedule a time to discuss your career aspirations with your current supervisor. Sometimes there are ways to reach bigger and better goals within your own company. Your company also might offer tuition reimbursement or some other incentive for continuing your education.

- [ ] Seek out a mentor. Is there someone whom you admire in the field you would like to work in? If so, ask if you can schedule a time to sit down and ask her questions.

 TIPS:

- Volunteer! One of the best ways to get experience if you don't already have it is to volunteer.

- If you are considering making a major career shift, job shadow someone in the career you are considering for a day or two to give you a true picture of what the work is like.

- Consider using a vision board to keep you on track with your goals.

- Always continue learning about your career. Read industry publications and blogs related to your field.

- Become well-read. Read books on a variety of subjects in a variety of genres in both fiction and nonfiction. Reading opens you up to new opportunities and helps you see things in new ways.

- If the industry you dream about working in is not very prevalent in your area of the country, consider a move. Change is good!

✔ STAY ORGANIZED!

Once a Month

☐ Take thirty minutes to catch up on the latest news in your industry by reading a trade publication or related blog.

☐ Read a book on any subject that interests you.

Every 3–6 Months

☐ Meet with your mentor or consult with your career coach.

☐ Check your progress on your list of goals. If there is something you've been putting off, break it down into a few more manageable goals and start working on them one at a time.

Once a Year

☐ Check for new educational programs that could benefit your career.

☐ Reevaluate your Strengths, Weaknesses, Opportunities, and Threats, and look for ways to improve your weaknesses.

NOTES:

Organize Your Resume & Cover Letter

Strong interview and people skills aren't the only things you need to land a job. You'll never get a chance to wow a hiring manager in person if your resume and cover letter are lacking.

Think of your resume as your own personal marketing profile. It should make it clear that you are a professional, responsible, intelligent person who would be perfect for the job you are applying for. If you are not computer savvy, you may want to hire a professional resume writer.

The cover letter is literally your first impression. Make it count! You probably have about one paragraph to do this. Don't assume that the person reading it will read the *entire* page (would you if you had two hundred resumes to get through?).

Tailor your cover letter to the position you are applying for and be sure to use keywords from the job posting. Companies that receive lots of applications often use computer programs to screen applications. These programs hit on keywords that were used in the job description, so if you leave these out, your resume may be disqualified without ever being read. Your cover letter should be altered with each job you apply for.

✔	THIS WEEK'S GOALS:
☐	Keep your resume under two pages in length, and do not use a font size smaller than ten points.
☐	Be sure your resume includes the following: • **Name and Contact Information:** Include your city of residence, phone number, e-mail, and website or blog URL if you have them. (Be sure your blog is error-free and

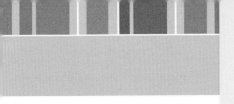

Organize your life around your dreams—and watch them come true.

—UNKNOWN

has a professional tone. Your resume may be perfect, but if the blog has typos, poor grammar, and mostly irrelevant personal content, you may not get a call). Also ensure your voice mail is professional and music-free.

- **Career Summary:** This should include the highlights of your career thus far, listed as bullet points immediately following your contact information.

- **Education:** List the name of your college or university, major and degree, and any specialties or minors. Any work-related seminars, courses, or workshops should also be included.

- **Keywords:** Research the job titles and keywords used in the descriptions of jobs you are interested in. Use these words in your resume, without overdoing it. Examples of keywords are specific software programs or specifically mentioned skills (for example, managing others).

- **Employment History:** Start with you most recent position and work backward for the past fifteen years. Point out any accomplishments or achievements you had. Also include the skills you possess. It's important to quantify your achievements (e.g., awarded the best salesperson in the district out of twenty-five other contenders; established a safety program in compliance with state, federal, and OSHA regulations; received "exceeded expectations" three consecutive years).

- **Professional Memberships and Interests:** Include hobbies, volunteer work, and anything else that proves you are a well-rounded person.

☐ Consider leaving the following information out of your resume:
- Anything that will reveal your age, including your date of birth and the year you graduated.
- Specific dates of employment if you were at a company for less than a year.
- Outdated skills or computer programs. Make sure your skills are up-to-date.
- "References available upon request." Employers know you will provide them if you are asked to.

☐ Have your resume proofread by at least two people who excel at grammar and spelling. Give them plenty of time to review it so they are not rushed. Proofread your resume yourself, carefully reading each word. Pay careful attention to areas you revised because you may have forgotten to delete a word or change a verb tense.

☐ Craft your cover letter so it gives hiring managers a glimpse of what you have to offer without repeating what they will read on your resume. Try to sound as original as possible.

☐ Start the body of your cover letter with a reference to the specific job you are applying for, including a reference number if possible. Also include this reference number and/or title in the subject line if you are e-mailing your resume.

☐ Mention how you found out about this opening. If you have a professional connection to someone at the company, mention this in the cover letter. Be sure to clear it with your contact first, because the hiring manager likely will contact that person.

☐ Write a paragraph or two explaining what you can bring to this position and how you can specifically benefit the company.

Include ways you will fit their needs, specifically referring to areas mentioned in the advertisement or job posting.

☐ Briefly explain what you admire about the company and why you want to work there. Be sincere and specific about positive qualities you have researched.

☐ Thank them for their time, and be sure to state that you have enclosed your resume for their review. Your cover letter should be fewer than three hundred words.

NOTES:

TIPS:

- It's unprofessional to use a "nickname" e-mail address on your resume (such as luvbug or koolkat). Use one that includes your name (such as firstname.lastname@gmail.com), even if it is a temporary one you set up just for your job search.

- Be sure your resume is easy to read. Use different font sizes and bold print for headings, and make lists bulleted or numbered, but avoid using a variety of fonts. Use something standard, professional, and readable such as Times New Roman or Arial. Be consistent with the way you format headings and lists.

- Consider a unique format for your resume, something different that will catch the hiring manager's eye and show him that you are a unique person, but don't compromise readability.

- Tailor your resume specifically to the position. Don't create one standard resume to send to all positions. Make adjustments for each job to add keywords and play up specific strengths.

- *Never* send your resume as an e-mail attachment titled "resume. doc." Always title it with your name such as "Jennifer Ford Berry. doc." Not only will you stand out, but many employers will delete e-mails with the first title.

- In today's business world, it is more appropriate to close your cover letter with "All the best" or "Kind regards" instead of "Sincerely."

- Continue to update your resume even while you are steadily employed and not actively seeking a job. Update it each time you win an award, complete more training, receive a certification, master a new software, or take on a new responsibility at your current job. You never know when a new job opportunity will present itself.

✔ STAY ORGANIZED!

Once a Month

☐ Check in with anyone whom you have sent your resume to in the past month but have not heard back from.

Every 3–6 Months

☐ If you change addresses, be sure to update your resume and your cover letter.

☐ If you are steadily employed, use your midyear review to update your resume. Include new accomplishments and new responsibilities.

Once a Year

☐ If you include your photo on your resume, be sure to update to a current photo if the shot no longer looks like you.

☐ If you are steadily employed, use your annual review to update your resume. Again, include new accomplishments and new responsibilities.

☐ Update your volunteer work and hobbies to reflect any changes.

☐ Evaluate the skills you have listed and revise as necessary. Consider taking a training class to keep your skills up-to-date or to gain new skills. This investment will keep you competitive.

Organize Your Job Search

With the recent high unemployment rate, this chapter may be more important now than ever before. Or maybe you have a job, but you believe that your talents could be better used at a new place of employment. Or maybe you have decided to follow your passion and pursue a different line of work. Whatever the case may be, finding a good job is no easy task. Nearly 80 percent of job openings are never posted publicly. If you want to find out about a job opening, you need to network. Find a contact within the company you want to work for so you have an advocate who can give you a good recommendation and help you land an interview. I hope these tips make your search a little easier.

✔   THIS WEEK'S GOALS:

☐ Before you start your search, make sure your resume is up-to-date, proofread, and ready to go (see week 12). You need to be able to send out your resume as soon as you hear about a job.

☐ Be proactive by posting your resume online so employers can find you. Use sites such as LinkedIn, www.monster.com, and www.careerbuilder.com. Be sure to use keywords that will bring up your resume when people do an Internet search for candidates in your field. Your resume may get you noticed, but most likely you will need to contact companies directly.

☐ Dedicate at least two days per week to finding links and resources specifically related to your industry. These could be trade publications and associations, mailing lists, discussion boards, etc. Interact with the resources and use them to help you find job leads. Schedule this time in your planner and treat it like a job itself.

Begin somewhere; you cannot build a reputation on what you intend to do.

—LIZ SMITH

☐ Tell everyone you know—family, friends, and former colleagues—that you are looking for a new job. Describe the kind of position you are looking for and offer to send them your resume. Ask them if they know of any positions where they work.

☐ Contact the career services office at your college and see what services they can offer you. Also check with the alumni association for potential contacts in your industry.

☐ Identify companies (either locally or nationally) that you would like to work for and check their websites daily for new job postings. Periodically call their human resources department to check for open positions.

☐ Set up an Excel spreadsheet or a notebook to record which companies you have contacted. Include columns for the following: date of initial contact, contact names, notes, follow-up dates, and scheduled interviews. You will feel much more in control and motivated if you are tracking your efforts and planning out your week.

☐ Use all of the social media outlets to give you leverage in the job hunt. Use Twitter, LinkedIn, and Facebook to network with potential employers and other people who are working in the industry you want to be in. See week 20 for more on how to organize your social media presence and message.

☐ Subscribe to your college's alumni online newsletter or quarterly magazine.

TIPS:

Contact the company within a week of submitting your resume. Find contact information for the human resources department on the company's website. Send an e-mail, make a phone call, or call reception. In a stack full of resumes, hiring managers are looking for standouts. After the initial contact, follow up every other week.

- Think twice before hiring a professional recruiter. Due to the economic downturn many companies are not using professional recruiters. Instead companies are posting positions on websites and instituting employee referral programs to discover new talent.

- Many people find the request of "return receipts" and "confirmations" to be rude and may delete your e-mail in response.

- One of the biggest mistakes people make when they get laid off is not starting their job search fast enough. Start looking for a new job as soon as you receive notice you're being let go, even if your current employer has offered to let you work for another few weeks or months.

- Your local library and unemployment office have additional resources that may help you in your job hunt. Also check with the career services department of your college.

- Consider joining a professional organization in your field to further your networking connections.

- If you want to work for a certain company, check out their website. Most sites have a Careers tab.

- Go to www.careeronestop.org to find government jobs that are available in your state.

STAY ORGANIZED!

Once a Month

☐ Check in with friends and former colleagues to see if they've heard of any new leads. Be sure to reciprocate and don't just use them for information.

Every 3–6 Months

☐ Update your resume and repost it online.

Once a Year

☐ Renew memberships to professional organizations.

NOTES:

Organize Your Interview Skills

You can never be too prepared for an interview. The best advice I can give is don't procrastinate! Be sure to do your research and prepare yourself well in advance. You'll have less stress on the day of the interview and feel more confident, which will come across in the interview. In addition to being on time and wearing appropriate attire, the keys to nailing the interview are researching the company and the position, knowing your resume, and preparing your questions.

✔	THIS WEEK'S GOALS:
☐	Be strategic when researching the company. Focus on mastering an understanding of these basic facts:

- company description
- products/services it offers
- customers/clients of the company
- what industry it operates within
- brief history of the business
- names of top executives
- company mission statement
- any current situations that are taking place within the business that may affect you or the company as a whole
- any current situations that are taking place within the industry that may affect the company (downward trends, new legislation or regulations, unstable competitors or rapidly growing competitors, etc.)

☐	Read over the company website, blog, and Facebook fan page.
☐	Prepare a list of questions. The interview isn't just for the employer to see whether you are a good fit for the company; it's also

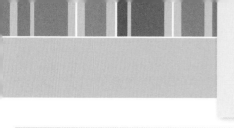

*In business, you don't get
what you deserve, you get
what you negotiate.*

—CHESTER L. KARRASS

for you to see whether this position is a good fit for you. Consider
asking the following questions:

- What types of tasks would I be doing during a typical
  workday?
- What are the hours for this position?
- Is there any travel involved?
- What are the opportunities for advancement?
- What are your expectations for this position?
- What do you like most about your job?
- What will my on-board process look like?
- How soon can I start?

☐ Carefully read over the resume you sent the company to refresh
your memory.

☐ Rehearse your answers, either by yourself or with someone you
trust. Some standard interview questions to practice are:

- Why do you want this job?
- What specific skills can you bring to this position?
- What ideas or goals would you bring to this position?
- What are your biggest strengths and weaknesses?
- Where do you see yourself in five years?
- What was your favorite job from your past?
- Why did you leave your last position?
- How do you respond to deadlines? Describe a time
  when you missed a deadline.

☐ Do a practice interview by yourself while sitting in front of a full-
length mirror. Pay attention to your body language. Work on pre-
senting a friendly, pleasant demeanor, and avoid fidgeting.

☐ Prepare an "elevator speech"—a three-minute personal and professional summary of yourself.

☐ Regardless of how casual the environment is, dress to impress! Suits are always a safe bet regardless of the company or position. Avoid cleavage-revealing clothing, sandals, shorts, or skirts more than two inches above the knee. Your appearance should be free of facial hair, visible tattoos, multiple piercings, and radical hair color.

☐ Tell your references about your interview. Confirm that they are still willing to be a reference and that you have their most current contact information. Type up your reference list and bring two copies, printed on resume-quality paper, to the interview.

☐ The night before, press your clothes and pack your briefcase. Include two copies of your resume and references, two black ink pens, work portfolios, and directions. Organize your briefcase in case you have to pull something out of it during an interview.

☐ Be prepared to explain any gaps in your resume. If you put your career on hold to raise your children, be confident and take credit for your accomplishments outside of the workforce.

 TIPS:

- At the end of the interview, express your interest in the position and ask for the job.

- Don't ask about salary, benefits, time-off policies, or holidays in the first interview.

- Write a handwritten thank-you note to each of the people who interviewed you in person.

- Give yourself at least thirty extra minutes of travel time in case of traffic or parking issues. If you are very early, wait in your car. Check in with reception about ten minutes before the interview.

- Turn your cell phone off prior to entering the interview.

- When you meet the person interviewing you, look him directly in the eye when you shake his hand.

During the interviewing process, remain positive and professional. Do not speak badly of your former job or supervisor.

Be prepared for an interview at a moment's notice. Gigi DeGaine-Roland specifically liked to catch people off guard and would start the interview process the moment the candidate picked up the phone when Gigi called to schedule a formal interview.

✔	STAY ORGANIZED!
	Once a Month
☐	Stay on top of industry news by reading business-to-business publications, professional blogs, and business reports.
	Every 3–6 Months
☐	Practice your interviewing skills with a mock interview (even if you're secure in your work).
	Once a Year
☐	Evaluate your professional wardrobe. Does your interview suit still fit? Is it in good repair?
☐	Consider going on at least one interview in your field to stay updated on what employers are looking for in your industry.

Organize Your Image

Like it or not, we are constantly being judged. In our private lives we can be secure in expressing our individualism, and hopefully we have the self-esteem to be ourselves and not let others' opinions weigh us down. But in the working world we need to project a positive image that is in line with the companies for which we work (or for which we desire to work).

While it's important to align with your company's goals, you still want to stand out for all the right reasons. Branding yourself will help you focus on attributes that make you stand out in the workplace. As you begin to shape your image, take time to consider what you are really good at. What are your strengths and what are your weaknesses? Think positive to look positive. Who are you and what do you stand for? These are the key questions to ask yourself. The bottom line is this: If you know yourself well and are proud of the person you are, it will be easier to talk about yourself.

✔ THIS WEEK'S GOALS:

☐ Practice acting a little more enthused than you really feel. You don't need to be a cheerleader, and you don't want to seem insincere. Practice subtle, positive facial expressions in the mirror, such as slightly raising your eyebrows to show interest and giving a closed-mouth smile to show that you agree. Maintain good eye contact (without staring). Keep your body language open. Avoid crossing your arms, furrowing your eyebrows, or frowning.

☐ Whether you are standing, sitting, or walking, be conscious of your posture. Good posture exudes confidence. No slouching! Keep your shoulders and hips parallel.

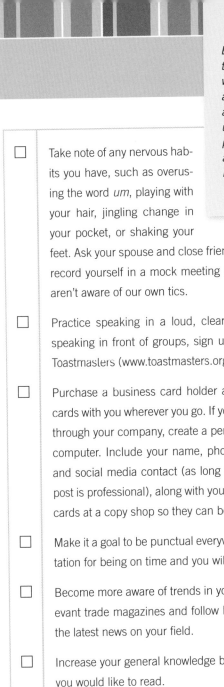

> *Each one of us holds the promise of greatness within our hearts, minds, and souls. Our potential and where it leads us are unique as our fingerprints, yet the way to access what is possible is universal.*
>
> —MARIANNA OLSZEWSKI

☐ Take note of any nervous habits you have, such as overusing the word *um*, playing with your hair, jingling change in your pocket, or shaking your feet. Ask your spouse and close friends for objective opinions, or record yourself in a mock meeting or mock interview. We often aren't aware of our own tics.

☐ Practice speaking in a loud, clear voice. If you have trouble speaking in front of groups, sign up for a speech class or join Toastmasters (www.toastmasters.org).

☐ Purchase a business card holder and carry your most current cards with you wherever you go. If you don't have business cards through your company, create a personal business card on your computer. Include your name, phone number, e-mail address, and social media contact (as long as all of the information you post is professional), along with your areas of expertise. Print the cards at a copy shop so they can be professionally trimmed.

☐ Make it a goal to be punctual everywhere you go. Have the reputation for being on time and you will earn people's respect.

☐ Become more aware of trends in your industry. Subscribe to relevant trade magazines and follow blogs and websites that have the latest news on your field.

☐ Increase your general knowledge base by making a list of books you would like to read.

TIPS:

- Whether you are networking or speaking with co-workers, be discrete about what you share. Avoid sharing too many details about health issues, romantic relationships, or personal problems. Avoid sensitive subjects such as religion, politics, and finances. Be aware of who is around you. If a co-worker is also a close friend, call her after work to discuss personal issues or go out to lunch (somewhere outside of your office building) to discuss them.

- If you work in a cubicle or in very close proximity to others, avoid making personal phone calls at your desk. If you must make calls during work hours, do so on your lunch break from the privacy of your car.

- Whenever you are at a work-related event or party, be very conscious of your dress and your behavior. One night of drunken indiscretion can cause even the most respected person in the office to lose all of the respect he has worked hard to earn.

- Try to have about eighteen inches of personal space around you when you are talking or networking with other people.

- Smile! This will help you feel more at ease and you will look more confident.

- Try to be as helpful as possible. If you can't do a job, clearly state why you can't, and if the job or question should be directed elsewhere, redirect the person to the correct contact in a friendly way.

 Dress appropriately for your position or the position you want to have. Unfortunately people are judged by the way they look.

 When you start your job, avoid office gossip and keep conversations with co-workers light and work-related.

Once a Month

☐ Refill your business card holder.

☐ Read a current trade magazine for your industry to stay on top of new trends.

Every 3–6 Months

☐ Make sure you are keeping up with your reading list.

☐ Attend at least one event related to your profession.

Once a Year

☐ Schedule a consultation with your hairdresser and evaluate your hairstyle. If it is still working for you, great. If you need a change, talk to the stylist about your options and what style would look best on you. If you are stuck in a rut, you may need to find a new hairdresser with more modern ideas and stronger skills.

☐ Reorder your business cards if you are getting low.

NOTES:

Organize Your Professional Development

To stay competitive in today's job market, it's important to stay up-to-date on the latest practices and new knowledge in your field. Some professions require continuing education to maintain licenses and certifications. Specialty certifications, post-secondary degrees, and advanced training will help you receive pay increases and promotions. It's important to make time for this professional development.

✔ THIS WEEK'S GOALS:

☐ If your profession requires continuing credits to maintain your license or certification, make sure you know the requirements. Explore the options you have available for receiving these credits and identify programs that will work with your schedule. Register early for extra discounts.

☐ Explore voluntary training and certifications you can receive for your profession. Check with professional societies, unions, and your co-workers and human resources department.

☐ Consider enrichment courses that can help you stay up-to-date in your industry.

☐ Research professional organizations you could join. These organizations often offer great networking opportunities and publications covering the latest news in your industry. They may also offer training opportunities and continuing education credits for attending meetings and seminars.

☐ Schedule a time to speak with your supervisor or human resources department about professional development. Ask what certifications or accreditations would help you earn more money or

If you don't know what your passion is, realize that one reason for your existence on earth is to find it.

—OPRAH WINFREY

receive a promotion. Present any programs you have researched and are interested in, and ask if these program would help improve your position with your company. Also inquire about any tuition assistance programs that your company may offer to promote professional development.

☐ If you are going to go back to school, set up a research schedule for evaluating different schools. Applying to college and graduate programs can be expensive and time-consuming. Avoid wasting both by doing your research *before* you apply. Visit the campus. Meet with professors and students. Ask for details about their admission standards. You want to apply to programs that you have a good chance of getting into.

☐ Schedule any testing (GRE, MCAT, LSAT) you need to complete to apply for admission to programs.

☐ Spend some time researching scholarships and grants. It may even be beneficial to hire a grant writer.

☐ Consider an online campus. Distance learning can be convenient and inexpensive if you still need to hold down a job. Attending this type of school also opens up your geographic options, which can be helpful if your program is not offered locally.

☐ Take advantage of lowering your income taxes while in school. Take the Hope Credit for up to $1,800 per year for the first two years of college. If you don't qualify for the Hope Credit, take the Lifetime Learning Credit for up to $2,000 on any post-secondary education.

TIPS:

- If you will work and go to school at the same time, find a program that is tailored for working adults.

- Consider completing a certification even if your current job won't give you a promotion or pay raise for completing it. It will make you more competitive in the job market and may open the door to a new job.

Keep up-to-date on your profession and be familiar with the latest technology, laws, and other pertinent information. Continue to develop yourself by taking self-paced training courses, studying for a higher certification level, and taking management courses. Prove you want to better yourself.

NOTES:

STAY ORGANIZED!

Once a Month

☐ Catch up on the latest news in your industry by reading trade publications and blogs.

☐ Organize and file your training certificates. Log your continuing education credits.

Every 3–6 Months

☐ Register for certification classes or seminars you need to complete.

☐ Research any enrichment courses that are available.

Once a Year

☐ Renew your memberships to professional organizations.

☐ Attend a conference related to your industry.

☐ Renew any certifications that are about to expire.

Organize an Extended Leave From Work

There are many reasons you may need to take an extended leave from work, such as continuing education, pregnancy, extended travel, surgery, research, mental health, caregiving, etc. In order to get the most out of your time off, whether it's for enrichment or recovery, you need to feel good about the way you leave the office. You need to know that things will be properly managed while you are gone and that you won't be absolutely buried when you return. This week will help you set up a successful leave of absence from your job.

✔	**THIS WEEK'S GOALS:**
☐	Interview at least two other people who have taken an extended leave from work and ask their advice. What did they do? How should you set this up? What did they learn from their leave? Would they do it again?
☐	You should start planning your leave as soon as you are aware of the need for it if it's for medical reasons (including pregnancy) or caregiving. If you are taking a sabbatical for travel or enrichment, start planning at least one year in advance and speak with your boss to find out if this is even an option. Ask about the guidelines and the process that you will need to follow.
☐	Begin recording all of the tasks that others will need to take on while you are gone. Write a description of each task and provide step-by-step instructions.
☐	Work with your supervisor to identify who will cover for you while you are gone. Begin training these people as soon as possible so they are prepared for when you are gone.

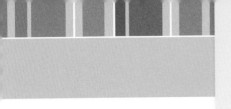

Sometimes it's the smallest decisions that can change your life forever.

—*KERI RUSSELL IN* FELICITY

☐ Identify projects that you would like to complete before you leave so they don't weigh on your mind while you are gone and so you can come back with a fresh start.

☐ About two weeks before you leave, begin notifying your contacts outside of the company of your absence. Introduce them to their temporary contact person.

☐ If possible, the week before you are scheduled to leave, have people practice as if you were already gone. This will give them time to ask questions and see how the new responsibilities will fit into their schedules. It will also give you time to wrap up projects and set things up for a smooth return.

☐ Set up automated systems for as many administrative tasks as possible before you leave.

☐ If you must check in with work and handle urgent situations during your leave, decide before you leave how much time you are willing to spend checking in and handling issues. Three hours per week should be enough. Set clear boundaries and let others know what you will and won't take care of. Remember, you are on leave, not working from home or another location. Use your time off for yourself.

☐ Write down your goals for this leave. What do you hope to get out of this? Do you want to reevaluate your life? Research other career paths? Take a long vacation? Write a book? Whatever it is, make your goals clear so you know your leave was worth the time off when it is over.

TIPS:

- Clean your desk and complete all of your filing before you leave. Returning to a clean, orderly desk will help you transition and keep you from feeling overwhelmed on your first day back.

- A week before you return to work, begin to adjust your body back to a work schedule. Go to bed at your typical workday bedtime and get up at your workday wake-up time.

- If you are taking maternity leave, interview day-care providers before the baby arrives. Start taking your child to day care a week before you are scheduled to return to work (following what will be your typical morning routine) so you have time to practice and adjust.

- Transition back to work gradually. A week before you go back, begin checking your e-mail. Start with just fifteen minutes a day, and add five minutes each day so you're caught up before you return.

NOTES:

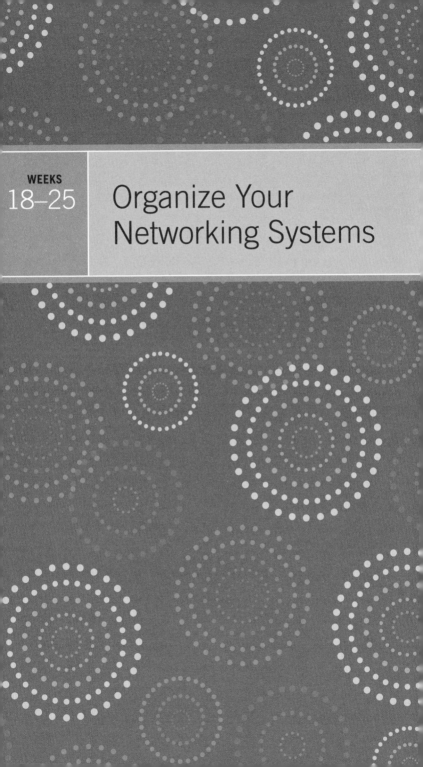

WEEKS 18–25

Organize Your Networking Systems

Organize Your Message

The word *message* can have a lot of different meanings. The message I'm referring to in this week is your professional message. It's what makes you or your business different from everyone else. What can you offer that will help you stand out in the crowd? What do you want people to know about you or your business? Once you identify what your message is, you will want to communicate it quickly and make it stick in people's minds.

A business owner can immediately see the benefits of having a clear message, but how does a message help someone in the corporate world or workforce? A message will help you sell yourself in professional circles. When you network or interview for a job, you'll be able to share a short, memorable message about yourself that will stick in people's mind.

Identifying your message may seem intimidating, but in my own life, I've found that if you can identify your purpose, creating and transmitting your message will be simple. Let's get started.

✔	THIS WEEK'S GOALS:
☐	Write down everything you can think of that makes you or your business unique.
☐	Interview five people with whom you network or do business. Ask them why they network or do business with you. Ask them to identify what attracts them to you. Ask them what they think your unique qualities are.
☐	Decide on and commit to a unique position that still aligns with your personal values and priorities. Think creatively. How can

Small business owners ... find motivation in a great cause or reason for being and connecting that great cause can become the drive to play the game at the highest level.

—JOHN JANTSCH

you do things different, and better, than someone else? It may be as simple as letting more of your personality shine through.

☐ Create a marketing purpose statement. This should be the way you want to be perceived in plain English—not a polished marketing message. It should state why you do what you do—your purpose—so you refer to it when you ask yourself, "Am I on my purpose?" Here's an example of my marketing purpose statement as a professional organizer: "I don't just want to help people get organized, I want to help them realize that clutter is preventing them from living the lives they were born to live. I want my services to be the lifeline they need and deserve."

☐ Distill your marketing purpose statement into a simple, straightforward core message that you can begin using in all of your marketing materials if you are a business owner, or use it on your resume and social networking sites if you are in the workforce. For example, Disney's core message is that it is the happiest place on earth.

☐ Use this core message to come up with a statement that you can use when talking to people about what you do and who you are. In other words, this will be your "talking logo," something you say that conveys your message and leaves people wanting to know more.

TIPS:

- Find a unique angle for your services or your business. You can't rely on price alone.

- Consider implementing a radical but quantifiable and not subjective guarantee to your customers, something that no other business is offering, and then stand behind it.

- To come up with a great message, consider the following: a problem you solve, a unique habit, your values, ways you provide great customer service, or a memorable personality.

- Before you launch a new message, test it out with trusted colleagues, your mentor, and select people in your networking group. Be sure to include the five people you interviewed. Ask for honest feedback.

- Aim to make your message timeless so it will last for years. A consistent message will help build your brand.

- Avoid buzzwords, jargon, or trendy words in your message so it doesn't seem dated or too "insider."

NOTES:

✔ STAY ORGANIZED!

Once a Month

☐ Practice living your message and speaking it to everyone you meet.

Every 3–6 Months

☐ Ask people you network with about ways you can improve yourself, and then work on their suggestions. Also ask them to point out what they think you are doing right so you can keep doing that.

☐ Consider sending a survey to your customers so you can receive feedback.

Once a Year

☐ Plan some time to evaluate your message. Is it still the message you want to convey, or have your values and goals changed over the past year? If changes need to be made, tackle them now.

Organize Your Website

If you own a business or sell a product or service, it is imperative that you have a website. We live in a time where most customers will search and read about you on your website before they step foot in your door or pick up the phone. A website should tell potential customers what you offer and help them get to know you, like you, and trust you.

If you do not already own a website, spend some time thinking about what you would like your site to look like. Look at your competitors' websites for an idea of the information they include. Check a variety of other sites to find ones that appeal to you. Bookmark them so you can refer to them. Then decide whether you can build the site yourself or need to hire a professional.

✔	THIS WEEK'S GOALS:
☐	Purchase a domain name. Your domain name should be short, relevant to your business, and easy to remember. If possible, include a keyword related to your business in your domain name.
☐	Decide on an Internet service provider and set up an account.
☐	If you will build the site yourself, set deadlines for when the work needs to be done. Set several small deadlines that allow you to work on it over time and see progress. Set a final deadline for when you want the site to go live so you are motivated to finish the work. If you are hiring someone, interview people and set deadlines for the person you hire.
☐	Make sure your website has great search engine optimization (SEO). Internet search engines rank search results based on how closely the content of a site matches the search words. Load your

Your website can become the marketing tool that holds all of your other marketing activities together.

—JOHN JANTSCH

site with terms your potential customers would search for. Include these terms on as many different pages of your site as possible. If you are looking to hire a Web designer, be sure to ask the person about his knowledge of search engine optimization before you hire him. A professional should be an expert at SEO.

☐ If you will accept payments on your website, obtain a merchant account for accepting credit cards or set up a PayPal link.

☐ Set up a link to a mailing list, a newsletter subscription, a Twitter account, and/or a Facebook page to capture contact information from your website visitors. Do whatever it takes to keep in touch with these potential customers.

☐ Make sure your navigation is simple. Place a link to every page on your home page. Place links within pages to other pages to make sure visitors can bounce around with ease.

☐ Make sure your contact information is easy to find, but never post your home phone number or home address. Use only business contact information on the site. If you need to, set up a separate phone line in your home that is for business use only.

☐ Include an "about me" page with a brief bio so people will know who created and runs the website.

☐ Create a separate general queries e-mail account for the website so your personal work account doesn't get flooded with spam. Set up strong spam filters for this account and check it daily.

☐ Make sure information readers may want to print will fit on a standard piece of paper without going off the margins.

TIPS:

- A good way to see if your website is simple enough to navigate is to let a six year old test drive it.

- Search engines will give your site a higher ranking if you have other websites in your industry linked to it, so make connections in your industry and share links with them.

- Your website should not just be a carbon copy of your company's brochure! It should offer value, educate prospects, and somehow provide interaction between you and your visitors.

- There are hundreds of websites out there that offer tracking widgets and devices so you can monitor your Web traffic. Do an Internet search to view your options. One that I personally love and use is Google Analytics, www.google.com/analytics. You must register for a Google account to access this page. Some statistics to track include:

  Visits: How many visitors have come to your site

  Page views: How many total pages have been viewed on your site

  Pages/Visit: How many pages on your site an average visitor visits (more is better)

  Bounce Rate: How many visitors left your site at the first page they viewed (less is better)

  Average Time on Site: How long an average visitor stays on your site

  Percent of New Visits: The percentage of your total visitors who are first-time visitors

Once a Month

☐ Take a close look at the statistics for your website. Where is your traffic coming from?

☐ If you are part of an affiliate program, track and record your earnings.

☐ Send out a newsletter.

Every 3–6 Months

☐ Have a mentor, co-worker, or friend look over your website and give you honest feedback.

☐ Update the pages, even if it's only to post new photos or share client testimonials.

☐ Check your SEO and look for ways to add more keywords to your pages.

Once a Year

☐ Renew your domain name.

☐ Renew the subscription to your website host company.

☐ Consider updating the look of your site if it's starting to look dated. Review colors and fonts.

Organize Your Social Media

Social networking is a powerful tool that is free. This week will show you how to use it to its full advantage and how to manage the amount of time you spend using it.

Decide if you want to distinguish your personal life from your professional life on social media sites such as Facebook. Do you want to keep your life private from potential customers, or do you want to share your interests with them?

✔	THIS WEEK'S GOALS:

☐ If you choose to create a separate page on Facebook for your business, set up an account (which is similar to setting up a new profile). Choose the best classification for your business (there are different categories).

☐ Add your logo in place of a photo if you have one.

☐ Go to the Notes tab. If you have a blog, you can pull your RSS feed through to the Notes page on Facebook.

☐ Upload photos and videos that represent your business, products, or services. If you have previously done this on YouTube, you can push your videos from there to your page. TubeMogul is an online service that also will allow you to post one video on many services.

☐ Use the Event tab to add any upcoming events, sales, appearances, or promotions your business is holding. Activate your Discussions tab if you want others to interact on your page.

☐ Choose a name for your business page that other employees can link to.

Social media involves a natural, genuine conversation between people about something of mutual interest, a conversation built on the thoughts and experiences of the participants.

—DAVE EVANS

☐ Be intentional with the time you spend on social networking. List goals, both professional and social, for your social media pages. For business owners, possibilities include:

- Follow trends in my industry
- Connect with potential customers
- Promote special offers

For individuals, possibilities include:

- Connect with family members, old friends, and new people who share my interests
- Follow trends in my industry
- Follow businesses I frequent for deals and promotion notifications

☐ Check your pages daily so you don't miss messages or questions from potential customers.

☐ Make full use of the functions to control your privacy and regulate who has full access to your complete profile.

☐ Search for friends, co-workers, family members, and more. Search your yearbooks and old company directories from jobs you have held if you need more names!

☐ Customize your news feed and following feed so you only receive notifications from people and businesses you truly want to stay up-to-date with. The more people in your news feed, the longer it will take you to read it. Remove feeds from games and other apps that are of no interest to you.

> ☐   Set time limits for how long you will be on a social media website. Have a time limit and objective for what you want to accomplish each time you log on, even if it's only to look at photos from a friend's trip. If you have problems staying focused, set a timer and force yourself to log off when it rings.

 TIPS:

- Always be professional when using social media, even when sharing personal information. Almost all hiring managers search applicant's social networking pages. And remember, what you post stays on servers and in archives even if you delete it from your page.

- Avoid making any references to a potential job or current job on social media. Many people have found themselves unemployed because of information they disclosed on social media or for using it when they should have been working. Be conscious of when you are posting and making changes to your sites.

- Post information that is interesting to you. Be authentic.

- Consider using a separate e-mail account designated for social media when you sign up for new accounts to avoid spam.

- Post a link to your blog if it relates to your career or business to let others know more about what kind of work you do and, therefore, what kind of work you could be hired for.

- Social media isn't about the content itself; it is about the conversations that result from the content.

- Add your social media links to your e-mail signature for added exposure.

STAY ORGANIZED!

Once a Month

☐ Update your news feed so you are receiving only the information you want.

☐ Connect with a friend you haven't spoken to in a while.

☐ Do a Google search of your name and see what comes up. Increase your privacy settings, defriend people, and remove content as needed based on what you find.

Every 3–6 Months

☐ Evaluate your friends and followers. Update your friends list as needed and, on your private account, remove friends and followers you don't interact with.

Once a Year

☐ Consider which social media networks are working for you and which are not. Some accounts may be worth deleting altogether rather than sitting stagnant.

NOTES:

Organize Your Blog

People blog for many reasons, and blogs can be personal or professional. They can be used to keep in touch with long-distance friends and relatives, to express opinions, or to document a project or metaphorical or physical journey. They are also a great marketing tool and an excellent way to establish yourself as an expert in your field. By now, most people know what a blog is, but if you aren't familiar with them, I will explain it as simply as possible. A blog is basically a website that:

- has regularly updated content (called posts)
- has a syndication feed that readers can subscribe to in order to be notified when new posts are placed on the blog
- allows for conversation—readers can comment anytime on the content

Blogs need to be carefully managed so they continue to serve their purpose (whether it's for fun or business) and don't take up a huge amount of time.

✔	THIS WEEK'S GOALS:
☐	Write out a list of reasons you want to blog.
☐	Using your list from the first goal, decide on the topic/niche of your blog. If you own a business or want to establish yourself as a leader in your industry, write about subjects related to your work. If it is a personal blog, write about things that interest you.
☐	Establish a budget for your blog. It's easier to start small. You can easily blog for free, and you may want to do that until you build a larger audience and can justify spending money on the blog.
☐	Choose a host for your blog. The most popular hosts are Blogger and WordPress. Think about your long-term goals, budget, and

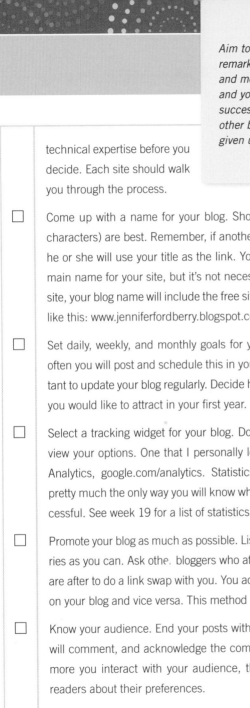

> *Aim to be unique, remarkable, compelling, and most of all, useful, and your blog will have success long after many other bloggers have all given up.*
>
> —CHRIS GARRETT

technical expertise before you decide. Each site should walk you through the process.

☐ Come up with a name for your blog. Shorter titles (under forty characters) are best. Remember, if another blogger links to you, he or she will use your title as the link. You can purchase a domain name for your site, but it's not necessary. If you use a free site, your blog name will include the free site's name and will look like this: www.jenniferfordberry.blogspot.com.

☐ Set daily, weekly, and monthly goals for your blog. Decide how often you will post and schedule this in your calendar. It's important to update your blog regularly. Decide how many new readers you would like to attract in your first year.

☐ Select a tracking widget for your blog. Do an Internet search to view your options. One that I personally love and use is Google Analytics, google.com/analytics. Statistics and comments are pretty much the only way you will know whether your blog is successful. See week 19 for a list of statistics to track.

☐ Promote your blog as much as possible. List it in as many directories as you can. Ask other bloggers who attract the audience you are after to do a link swap with you. You add the link to their sites on your blog and vice versa. This method is fast and free!

☐ Know your audience. End your posts with a question so readers will comment, and acknowledge the comments they leave. The more you interact with your audience, the better. Survey your readers about their preferences.

☐ Research affiliate programs that will let you earn commission. Find them by entering your niche + *affiliate programs* into your search engine.

☐ Be sure your blog has a subscription link so readers can keep up with your latest posts.

 TIPS:

- Find blogs that interest you, and then ask yourself why you find them appealing. How often do they add content? What don't you like? What would make you come back for more? How long are their posts? What is their writing style?

- Quality is better than quantity. The number one reason why people unsubscribe to a blog is because of too many posts, so don't feel pressure to write every day. When you post, make sure the content is strong.

- Keep your posts simple and limit it to one topic per post. The average reader will stay on your blog for ninety-six seconds. The experts recommend that your posts be at least 250 words and no more than one thousand words. Use lists, bold letters, colorful font, headings, pictures … whatever it takes to stand out and get the information across quickly.

- Don't let advertisements dominate your blog.

- Don't write a product review unless you have actually experienced the product.

Once a Month

☐ Check your goal list for your blog. Are you meeting or missing these goals? Write down steps you can take to meet these goals.

Every 3–6 Months

☐ Include a giveaway in one of your posts. Many times you can get someone to sponsor the giveaway in return for the free advertising and a link to their blog or website.

☐ Compare your blog's progress to others in your niche by visiting www.technorati.com and www.alexa.com.

☐ Write a few extra posts that you can save to use during a busy week when you don't have time to write.

☐ Send your readers a survey to find out what you should continue doing on your blog and what you should add or change.

Once a Year

☐ Renew your domain name.

☐ Review any affiliate programs you are a part of. Is the program still relevant to your blog? Has it generated any income? Is it worth keeping? Search for new affiliate programs as well.

NOTES:

_____

_____

_____

Organize Your Electronic Newsletter

An electronic newsletter is one of the most cost-effective ways you can communicate with potential customers. If you're not already taking advantage of this valuable resource, make it your goal to move more of your direct-to-consumer communications to a digital format this year. The goal for any electronic newsletter is to keep your name in front of prospects.

✔	THIS WEEK'S GOALS:
☐	Establish goals for your electronic newsletter. Will you use it for advertising, information, or offers of discounts and coupons?
☐	Determine how often you will send your newsletters. Weekly, fortnightly, monthly, or quarterly are a few options. Then set up a schedule for when the newsletter needs to go out and stick to it. Establish the delivery frequency with readers when they sign up so they know what to expect.
☐	Decide on the general topics your electronic newsletter will discuss. Possibilities include tips, business updates, sale information and coupons, and short, informative articles.
☐	Determine where you will find content. Will you write it all yourself? Will you work with contributors? If you plan to use other people's material, contact the original author before you use it, and credit the information appropriately.
☐	Decide where potential readers can sign up to be on your newsletter mailing list. Make it simple by setting up an automated link on your website, blog, or Facebook page. Be sure to list five benefits readers will receive from subscribing to your newsletter.

Online marketing is one of the most important ways you can market your goods, services, or overall business to potential customers.

—RHONDA ABRAMS

☐ Consider the digital platform you will use to send your newsletter. Some websites that offer the ability to send and maintain a digital newsletter are:

- www.constantcontact.com
- www.aweber.com
- www.myemma.com
- www.mailchimp.com
- www.verticalresponse.com

NOTES:

_____
_____
_____
_____
_____
_____
_____
_____
_____
_____
_____
_____
_____
_____
_____
_____

TIPS:

- Use small image files in your newsletter so it opens quickly and doesn't fill up recipients' Inboxes.

- Keep the content of your newsletter brief and easy to read. Use bulleted lists whenever possible.

- Fill your newsletter with links back to your website to generate more Web traffic.

- Work ahead on newsletter content and keep backup content on hand so you can easily maintain your delivery schedule.

- Don't send too many newsletters or electronic notifications, or people will consider your communications spam.

- Offer a free item or coupon as an incentive for people to sign up for your newsletter.

- Make it easy for newsletter recipients to forward the newsletter on to their friends and family.

- If you are sending your newsletter in an e-mail format, *always* list subscribers under BCC.

- Always use an interesting subject line.

✔	STAY ORGANIZED!

Once a Month

☐ Work ahead on newsletter content for the upcoming month.

Every 3–6 Months

☐ Evaluate the effectiveness of your newsletter. Does it increase your Web traffic or generate sales?

Once a Year

☐ Evaluate your number of newsletter subscribers for the year. What is your open rate and retention rate? How can you improve those?

NOTES:

_____

_____

_____

_____

_____

_____

_____

_____

_____

_____

_____

_____

Organize Your Direct Mail & Advertising

The right direct mail piece cannot only help you specifically target your ideal customer, but it can also provide a high return on investment. It's vital that you create a direct mail piece that is *very* personal and specific to the person or people you are mailing it to. A direct mail piece that does not pull in new customers will most likely not do any better in an expensive paid spot in a newspaper or magazine. Get your marketing right before you pay the big bucks.

Research the various companies and software programs available that can help implement and manage your mailing list. It often takes up to ten direct mailings to make an impression on a consumer. Don't give up after a few attempts.

✔ THIS WEEK'S GOALS:

☐ Make sure you have a successful mailing list to use. A successful list will target your ideal client, so start by creating a list of all the characteristics your ideal client would have. It should include geographic location, income, age, education, household size or number of employees (depending on whether you serve individuals or businesses), etc.

☐ After you've identified your ideal client, look into purchasing a list of names and addresses that matches it as closely as possible. InfoUSA offers mailing lists you can purchase.

☐ Set up a system that will help you log and organize any new contact's information, including information obtained from a purchased list. It doesn't matter whether you use a Rolodex, Excel spreadsheet or a program like ACT; the important thing is choosing a system that will be easy for you to use and maintain.

Your sales copy is meant to be a form of conversation with the reader ... Few things sound less sincere than when you try to be or sound like a really smart marketing person.

—JOHN JANTSCH

☐ Each time you send out a mailing, set up an Excel sheet or other tracking system to help you keep track of the results. The sheet should include a list of all the recipients, the date the mailing was sent, and the response rate. These sheets will help you further identify characteristics of customers who respond positively to your message.

☐ Schedule times in your calendar to call potential clients you need to follow up with after you have sent letters or marketing materials.

☐ Include the cost of postage and mailing pieces in your budget when buying a direct mail list.

NOTES:

_____

_____

_____

_____

_____

_____

_____

_____

_____

_____

_____

_____

TIPS:

- Understanding the culture of your target client is the key to finding the right mailing list for your business. Make sure you do not mail the right message to the wrong people.

- If you are not ready to buy a large mailing list, ask the company if they will waive the minimum and allow you to test a small portion of the list.

- Before you start any new marketing campaign, write down your specific goals for the campaign. Identify how many people you want to reach and how many leads you want to get from those people you contact. These goals will help determine the actions you need to take and will help measure the success of the campaign.

- You can collect mailing list information directly from potential clients on your website and social networking systems. Also be sure to send mailings to current and past customers.

- Always ask new customers how they heard about your business and keep track of their responses so you can track the effectiveness of your marketing efforts. If you offer a customer service survey, you can include this question on it.

- Offer potential customers incentives for responding to your mailing.

- When starting a direct marketing campaign, test your list first. Send out mail to a portion of your list to test the effectiveness of this method. You can even test a few different designs or colors to see which ones your customers respond to.

- When sending direct mail, include a deadline for action and an incentive for action to increase the speed of response.

✔ STAY ORGANIZED!

Once a Month

☐ Put in a call or e-mail to see if anything is new with a client or customer.

Every 3–6 Months

☐ Send out one direct mail piece.

Once a Year

☐ Plan out your marketing materials at the same time every year.

☐ Schedule dates when mailings will be sent throughout the year.

Organize Your Mobile Devices

Smartphones, laptops, and e-readers keep the world at our fingertips. How did we ever survive without them? These devices help us keep in touch with family and friends, and they also make it possible for us to work from just about anywhere. Some people seem to have their smartphones glued to their hands, and it can be hard to power down our electronics at night. It's important that you have a designated charging station for these devices so you always know where they are. Proper carrying cases will help you protect your investment, and proper time management skills will help you make the best use of these devices.

✔ THIS WEEK'S GOALS:

☐ Before you buy any electronic device, do your research. Technology advances so rapidly that your device may be outdated within six months of your purchase. Although you may want the newest gadget as soon as it appears on the market, if you wait for the second generation, you'll get more features and fewer glitches for your money.

☐ In your home, create one central charging station for your mobile devices. When you're not using a device, keep it in the charging station so you always know where it is. Keep all accessories, cords, and chargers in this station.

☐ Label one of your contacts in your phone ICE (In Case of Emergency), and connect this contact to your emergency contact person. Emergency responders may check your mobile phone to contact a loved one if you are incapacitated in an accident.

> *Man is still the most extraordinary computer of all.*
>
> —JOHN F. KENNEDY

☐ Set boundaries and follow proper etiquette with your mobile phone. Just because you have your phone with you at all times doesn't mean you have to answer every call as soon as you receive it.

☐ If your phone company does not provide a backup service for your contacts, make sure you do this on your own regularly. You can use Plaxo as an online Rolodex to keep track of all of your contacts' information.

☐ Regularly back up your laptop to a USB flash drive or an external hard drive. Keep these backup files in a single secure location in case your computer is lost or stolen.

☐ Keep your favorite websites tabbed and organized by setting up categories for them. Go to the top of your toolbar and click Favorites and then Organize Favorites.

NOTES:

TIPS:

- Consolidate your devices whenever possible. Do you need to carry three devices at the same time, or can you carry one that can serve the purpose of all three? Use one device to make calls and text, surf the Internet, and play music.

- If you are going to spend the money on a mobile communication device, get your money's worth and read the manual! You are not making the most of your investment if you do not know how to use the device to its full extent.

- Turn your phone off during family time and important meetings. Voice mail was made for a reason.

- Enter the number for customer service into your phone when you first get it.

- Save time by texting quick questions instead of calling.

- Install antivirus and spam protection software on your laptop so you are always protected. As soon as you purchase a new electronic device, put all the parts and manuals in a *labeled* resealable storage bag. This way you will always know which parts belong with which device, and if you ever get rid of it, you will know which pieces can go with it!

Once a Month

☐ Clean out your message Inbox on your cell phone. Lock messages that you need to save and don't want to accidently erase.

☐ Move important documents you are working on to a USB flash drive or external hard drive.

Every 3–6 Months

☐ Back up the contact names and numbers on your cell phone.

Once a Year

☐ Go through the contacts in your cell phone to update and organize them. Remove any that you no longer need and add new ones.

☐ Renew your antivirus software.

Organize Your Networking List

Networking is the most important tool that I have used for growing my businesses! Whether it is utilizing my social media outlets, attending a meeting, sending out a newsletter, or simply talking to a mom at a baseball game about what I do, I am constantly networking.

If you do it right, networking will lead to word-of-mouth advertising, which will lead to sales! But don't just push your own products. Help others network as well. People are more likely to speak positively of you and your products if you are doing the same for them.

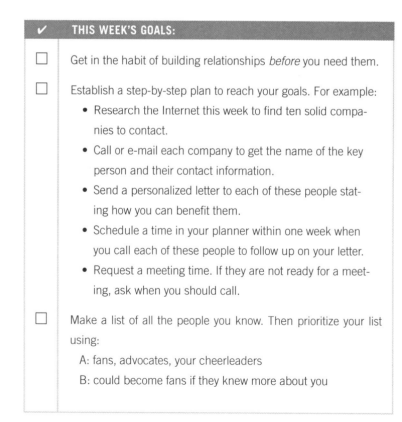

✔	THIS WEEK'S GOALS:

☐ Get in the habit of building relationships *before* you need them.

☐ Establish a step-by-step plan to reach your goals. For example:

- Research the Internet this week to find ten solid companies to contact.
- Call or e-mail each company to get the name of the key person and their contact information.
- Send a personalized letter to each of these people stating how you can benefit them.
- Schedule a time in your planner within one week when you call each of these people to follow up on your letter.
- Request a meeting time. If they are not ready for a meeting, ask when you should call.

☐ Make a list of all the people you know. Then prioritize your list using:

A: fans, advocates, your cheerleaders

B: could become fans if they knew more about you

Position yourself as a center of influence: the one who knows the movers and shakers. People respond to that, and you'll soon become what you project.

—BOB BURG

☐ Start your own networking group if you can't find one in your area that meets your needs. I once started a group for female business owners in Buffalo.

 TIPS:

Don't underestimate the power of networking at professional societies and in social settings.

- Whenever you make a networking connection, contact each person individually to make the contact personal. Group e-mails can be perceived as spam. Introduce yourself and say why you are initiating contact. Request a follow-up such as a phone call or e-mail, but give the recipient the choice of how to continue.

- Networking is a two-way street. Don't use people only for what they can give you. Share information with them. Learn about their needs and find ways to help them in return for the help they are offering you.

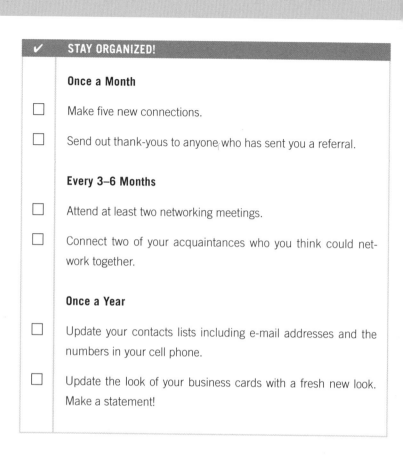

STAY ORGANIZED!

Once a Month

☐ Make five new connections.

☐ Send out thank-yous to anyone who has sent you a referral.

Every 3–6 Months

☐ Attend at least two networking meetings.

☐ Connect two of your acquaintances who you think could network together.

Once a Year

☐ Update your contacts lists including e-mail addresses and the numbers in your cell phone.

☐ Update the look of your business cards with a fresh new look. Make a statement!

NOTES:

Organize Your Work Spaces

Organize Your Home Office

Half of all American homes have a home office. Everyone benefits from having a designated workspace in their home, even if the work relates only to household duties such as bills and personal correspondence. You don't need to have a separate room designated as the office. You can use a hall closet or set up a desk in the corner of a common room such as the living room, kitchen, or family room. The important thing is that you have a permanent location for home-related clerical duties. And if you work from home, you need a secure place to keep all of your work-related material. The kitchen table should not be the designated space to work—it's not a permanent location.

✔	THIS WEEK'S GOALS:

☐ If you have not already designated a space in your home for an office, do so now. Ideally you want a space that:

- is large enough to hold everything essential to your work—even if it's only household-related
- is a place where you can concentrate
- motivates and inspires you to get your work done
- has electrical outlets for all of your equipment

☐ Decide on the functions of this space. Is it a space to do your career work? Do you pay your bills here? Do your kids do their homework in here? There's no right or wrong answer. Write down everything that happens here.

☐ Remove everything that does not serve the designated functions of this area. The home office often becomes a catchall for odds and ends that don't have a permanent home. Take these

It is easier to purchase products that denote superiority than to be actually superior in economic achievement.

—WILLIAM DANKO

items out of the room and find homes for them *after* you've finished organizing the office.

☐ Rearrange furniture so it is attractively arranged and makes it easy to work. Position your desk first. Ideally your work area should be set up in an L or U shape.

☐ Decide on shelving. Shelves are my favorite tools for increasing storage in a small space. They give you plenty of storage space without taking up any floor space.

☐ Evaluate the items you have left in your space. Donate or toss an item if you don't use it or love it. Try to combine or condense as much as possible. If you can store information on your computer, do so, and then get rid of the paperwork (or CDs in the case of a music collection). Group like items together and designate a home for each category.

☐ If you have children who constantly distract you or mess up your office, consider setting up a separate office space for them to work in. This could be a little table in the corner of your office or, better yet, a space that is not in your office at all. Giving them these boundaries will help them learn organizational skills.

☐ If you will be working from home or are self-employed, set up a schedule in your planner for your work hours in your home office. Set a start and end time for each day. Schedule time for lunch and for at least two fifteen-minute breaks to stretch, breathe, and even meditate.

TIPS:

- Set up a "To File" bin, box, drawer, or basket to hold files that you need to return to your filing cabinet.

- After you complete a large or rushed project, set aside time to organize your office. If you are in a hurry to meet a deadline or finish a project, chances are you may not take the time to put things in their "home." Organizing is a nice way to refocus your energy and prepare you for your next project. Plus you'll know your files for the completed project are complete and easy to find.

- Use sticky notes only for immediate reminders. Input important long-term information in a planner, on your computer, or in a project-related notebook so you don't lose it.

- If your office really needs a major makeover, pretend you are moving. Move everything out of the space and start over. Evaluate every item and piece of paper before you bring it back into the area.

- If you are short on space, purchase vertical rather than horizontal pieces of furniture.

- If you are starting an office from scratch, don't forget to measure! Measure the space and all furniture before you buy it.

- Adjust your chair height so you will be comfortable working.

- Consider track lighting to free up space on your desk.

- If you have a small space, lighter paint colors on the walls make a room look bigger.

✔ STAY ORGANIZED!

Once a Month

☐ File all papers in your "To File" bin.

☐ Shred confidential or personal information documents that you no longer need.

Every 3–6 Months

☐ Replenish office supplies that are running low.

☐ Reorganize your desk drawers and remove all of the items that you don't use or need.

Once a Year

☐ Remove all old files that you no longer need.

☐ Take a close look at the décor in your office and remove anything that you no longer use or love.

NOTES:

_____
_____
_____
_____
_____
_____
_____
_____

Organize Your Paper Clutter

When it comes to staying organized, papers are everyone's worst enemy. Why? Because more arrives on a near daily basis and it never stops coming. The good news is, it's less expensive and more practical to store as much information as possible in digital formats rather than on paper. It's easier to find what you are looking for in a digital format, and it's much easier to make changes to or update a digital document.

As much as possible, store information digitally to cut down on paper clutter. Follow this week's goals to organize and control any remaining paperwork. You can use this advice for the paperwork at your office and the paperwork in your home.

✔	THIS WEEK'S GOALS:

☐ Designate a spot in your home and your office for incoming and outgoing mail. If possible, have labeled containers (such as trays) for each category. Keep a recycling bin near your in-box.

☐ Decide on organizing containers that will work for you. Options include stacking trays, baskets, hanging files, files placed in staggered holders, and three-ring binders.

☐ Label your containers "Action," "To Read," and "To File," plus a container for each current project you are working on. You also may want a "To Do" container for paperwork that requires action, such as a signature, a bill to pay, or a review of benefits. When you place the paper in the "To Do" container, also note it as an A task on your to-do list (see week 6).

☐ Gather your most current paperwork, meaning today's mail and the contents of your mail table or in-box (or the first ten sheets if

Paper clutter isn't an organizing problem; it's a time-management problem.

—JULIE MORGENSTERN

you have a huge stack), and sort it into the appropriate container. Add "sort mail and paperwork" to your to-do list. This will be a permanent A task, something you should do every day. The more often you do it, the less time it will take.

☐ Recycle all junk mail as soon as you receive it.

☐ After you have your paperwork system in place, collect all the old papers scattered around your workspace. Make one large pile and work your way through it, sorting each paper into a pile based on category. If the paper goes with a current project, place it in the appropriate container. If it needs to be reviewed, place it in the "To Read" file. If papers are outdated and you no longer need them, recycle or shred them immediately. We only look at 20 percent of the paper we save, so push yourself to toss more than you think you can. Instead of creating a general "To File" pile that you will need to sort again, have different containers for each type of file you are creating or adding to. Make your file categories as general as possible so you don't have just one or two papers in a single file. Label each container for ease of use. If you have a huge stack, commit to working on it for ten minutes each day until it is gone.

☐ Place your files in a Bankers Box or filing cabinet. When setting up a file system, I use a straight-tab system and put the tabs one behind the other. Your eyes and fingers can follow along in a straight row instead of weaving back and forth. Consider a desktop storage device for those files you are currently working on.

TIPS:

- Reduce paper clutter by jotting notes, ideas, to-do's and other information in your day planner or on your daily or master to-do list.

- Force yourself to make a decision about how to handle a piece of paper the minute you touch it. Toss it or place it in your "To Do" or "To Read" file with a reminder on your to-do list right away.

- Place extremely important papers in a fireproof safety box.

- Shred any paper you are tossing that has your address, birth date, account number, or Social Security number on it.

- Remove your name from bulk mailing services. Visit www. dmachoice.org and www.stopjunkmail.org. Send a postcard with your name and address to Mail Preference Service, Direct Marketing Association, P.O. Box 643, Carmel, NY 10512-0643. Remove your name from the National Demographics and Lifestyles List by sending your name and address on a postcard to List Order Department, 1621 18th St., Suite 300, Denver, CO 80202.

- If the information can be found electronically, toss the paper!

- Toss files for large events after the events pass.

- Use this as a guide for what to keep and what to shred:
  ATM Receipts: Save only for taxes
  Credit Card Statements: Keep only the most current
  Insurance Policies and Bills: Keep only the most current
  Medical Bills: Keep for three years
  Mortgage: Keep for as long as you own the property
  Social Security Statements: Keep only the most recent annual
    report
  Tax Records: Keep for seven years

✔ STAY ORGANIZED!

Once a Month

☐ File the papers in your "To File" tray. If possible, toss the papers instead of filing. You may find you don't need them after all.

☐ Throw away any expired coupons.

☐ Add new business cards or contact information to your system.

☐ Make sure your incoming mail area is cleaned out.

Every 3–6 Months

☐ Weed through your files and toss any old, outdated, or unnecessary papers so your files don't become too large.

☐ Replenish mail supplies that are getting low.

Once a Year

☐ Cancel any magazine or newspaper subscriptions you have not been reading.

☐ Every January clean out your file folders. Move all paper that pertains to this particular tax year to an archive home such as a bin or box and label.

NOTES:

_____

_____

_____

_____

Organize Your Filing Systems

The key to keeping filing systems and paperwork organized is to create a system that is easy for you to understand and maintain. Most people don't want to file important papers because they are afraid they won't be able to find them again. That is why it is crucial that you keep a small number of distinct file categories.

As technology advances, we deal more and more with electronic documents and files and less with papers. This week's goals and tips apply to both your filing cabinet and your computer. To save space and paper, keep only electronic documents and opt not to receive (or print) paper copies.

✔ THIS WEEK'S GOALS:

☐ Evaluate your current filing system. What about it is working? What isn't working about it? What type of system will be easy for you to maintain?

☐ Create categories for your files. List the type of paperwork you keep, and then think about how you would look for that paperwork. Use your first instinct because that is what is most logical to you. Try to keep as few different files as possible. To achieve this, you may choose to lump all like things together, such as all information relating to your car—payments, maintenance, and insurance—in one file labeled "Car." Be as broad or as detailed as you like, but try to avoid creating files that will hold fewer than five pieces of paper. That's too tedious to deal with and takes up extra space.

☐ Type or write a master file list that reminds you of what category you put each paper under until you know this by heart. Use the

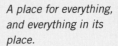

*A place for everything,
and everything in its
place.*

—PROVERB

specific titles that you will label each file with. (This is also handy if someone else will be using your files.) Paper Tiger software is a good resource that can help you with this. Do this whether you are using paper folders or electronic folders.

☐ Create new folders (paper or electronic) that are clearly label with the titles on your master file list.

☐ Gather all of your loose paperwork that needs to be filed and start filing. With each piece of paper, ask yourself, "Do I have more than an 80 percent chance of needing this again? And do I need to save this, or can I locate this information on the Internet if I need it in the future?"

☐ After you've filed your loose papers, go through your old files and purge them. Shred and recycle anything you no longer need. Move papers you are keeping to the appropriate new folder.

☐ Search your computer's hard drive and desktop for loose documents and move them to the appropriate folder. Go through all the old folders on your computer and move the files to the appropriate new folder.

☐ Collect all of your business cards, phone numbers, addresses on scrap pieces of paper, and return address labels that you are keeping for contact information, and input them into a digital address book, a physical address book, or a Roledex. Use only one system so it is easier to maintain and you don't miss a contact.

TIPS:

- Store small pieces of paper such as receipts in closed-sided folders or in labeled envelopes within a file folder so they don't slip out.

- Do not label a file *Miscellaneous*. You will never remember what you placed in there.

- Consider using a device with Bluetooth that will automatically sync with your phone and your computer.

- Try not to make folders for a category that will house fewer than five sheets of paper.

- When purchasing a filing cabinet, keep in the mind the weight of the files you will be storing and be sure the cabinet will be able to tolerate this weight.

- Be sure to have at least one drawer you can lock in your cabinet for important, confidential documents.

- Keep about five new, empty folders at the front of your filing system so that making a new file will be easy.

- Consider setting up a small desktop system for files or projects that you are currently working on.

- Purge your files whenever you add new paperwork that makes old paperwork obsolete.

- Whenever possible, choose an electronic document over a paper document. Export receipts for online payments to your computer instead of printing one.

STAY ORGANIZED!

Once a Week

☐ Add new contacts to your address system.

Once a Month

☐ File loose papers.

Every 3–6 Months

☐ If you are using a paper organizer for your contacts, make a photocopy of it for backup.

☐ Back up your digital files on an external hard drive or a flash drive.

Once a Year

☐ Purge each file of outdated information.

☐ Check your contacts to make sure they are still current.

NOTES:

_____

_____

_____

_____

_____

_____

_____

_____

Organize Your Computer

The principles behind organizing your computer are no different than organizing a bookcase or drawer. You need an efficient system that you can easily use and maintain, and *everything* needs a "home," even on your computer. Files, e-mail, important documents, and photos all need their own designated folders. Plus, the less clutter you keep on your computer, the more efficient it will run and the more storage space you will have for truly important documents.

USB flash drives are fantastic for not only backing up information on your computer but for storing information without taking up space. They also makes it very easy to transfer and transport information. If you have important documents, copy them to a flash drive, and place the drive in a secure location, such as a lockbox or fireproof box.

✔ THIS WEEK'S GOALS:

☐ If you haven't done so already, organize the files and documents on your computer following the advice in week 28.

☐ If you have a large amount of information saved on your hard drive, consider alternative homes for this information, such as a CD, a USB flash drive, or an external hard drive, to save space and keep your processor speed fast.

☐ Install or update antivirus programs and firewalls.

☐ Delete all temporary files you do not need.

☐ Improve your computer's performance by running a defragmentation program.

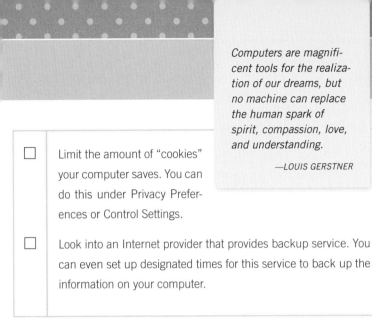

Computers are magnificent tools for the realization of our dreams, but no machine can replace the human spark of spirit, compassion, love, and understanding.

—LOUIS GERSTNER

☐ Limit the amount of "cookies" your computer saves. You can do this under Privacy Preferences or Control Settings.

☐ Look into an Internet provider that provides backup service. You can even set up designated times for this service to back up the information on your computer.

NOTES:

_____

_____

_____

_____

_____

_____

_____

_____

_____

_____

_____

_____

_____

_____

_____

_____

_____

TIPS:

- If you have a lot of large files on your computer, consider purchasing a program that will compress these huge files for you to save space on your hard drive or to allow you to move the items to a USB drive or CD. File compression can be done in a few seconds.

- Do not delete files or software on your computer unless you know what the software or file does and are 100 percent sure you don't need it. If you are not sure, move the file to a CD or flash drive and then, if your computer starts acting weird, you can replace the file.

- Use your computer desktop for items that you are currently working on, and then file them in your computer when you are done.

- Limit the names of file folders on your computer to fifteen characters. They are easier to understand at a glance—especially if you have to send them in an e-mail.

NOTES:

STAY ORGANIZED!

Once a Month

☐ Set up your antivirus programs to do a full system scan.

Every 3–6 Months

☐ Back up all of the files on your computer.

☐ Move all photographs on your computer to a flash drive or disk.

Once a Year

☐ Renew your antivirus/spam software.

Organize Your Professional Workspace

At your workplace, you may not have much control over the type (or quantity) of furniture you have in your workspace, and it may or may not be movable. This week will help you organize your work area to be efficient and comfortable regardless of these limitations. In an office setting, you need to be very aware of the message your desk is sending. If there are no personal effects and it looks like you could pack up your desk in less than two minutes, you may seem unapproachable and not invested in your work. On the other hand, too many personal items can be a distraction and seem un-professional. Find that careful balance, and when in doubt, tour your building and follow the example of the majority. A few framed photos or posters, a lamp, and perhaps a plant liven the space without overwhelming it.

Implement these goals one at a time on your own time so you don't lose productivity at work. You could come in thirty minutes early, stay thirty minutes late, or work on it over lunch. Organize one area at a time, for example one filing drawer per day or one shelf per day.

✔ THIS WEEK'S GOALS:

☐ Start by purging. Evaluate each item (including files and pieces of paper), and remove things that you don't use and don't belong in your work area. Remove all decorative items that you don't love. Remember, you can tackle this project one area at a time. Do one shelf or drawer per day until you purge them all.

☐ After you've finished purging, create categories for your items by placing like things together. All of your manuals could go together;

all of your pencils, highlighters, and markers together; and all of your sticky notes together. Then decide on the best place to house each category. Use containers, bookends, or drawer dividers to help keep categories separate and tidy. Consider setting up your office in zones. This will help you visualize where things should go.

☐ Completely clear off your desk and place everything on the floor. Clean the desktop area thoroughly. Evaluate each item before you return it to your desktop. Place items that you use most frequently within arm's reach of where you sit. If you have to get up to put something away, chances are you won't! File things as needed. Place items in an appropriate category if possible. Try to keep your desk as clear as possible. Gather the loose pieces of paper and input the information into your calendar, contact list, or project file as needed. In the future, immediately enter this information into the appropriate place to avoid collecting scraps of paper.

☐ Place two trays or baskets on your desk for an in-box and out-box. Clearly label both and place them where people can easily put things in your in-box.

☐ If you frequently pull files to reference or receive lots of paperwork that needs to be filed, designate a "To File" bin and use it to collect all of the items you need to file. Set aside time each week (or each day) to clear this bin. This is a great activity to do at the end of the day, especially on a Friday, so you have a clear desk at the start of the next week.

- [ ] If you keep files for your current projects on your desk, be sure that you have holders or bins to keep them tidy and easy to access. Consider vertical wire holders or wall-mounted holders.

- [ ] If you work on projects that involve lots of paperwork that doesn't easily fit into a file, use copy paper boxes. Clearly label one box per project. Stack them in your workspace or, if available, keep them in an open bookcase. If you need more shelving, speak with your manager.

- [ ] Make a "Need Follow-Up" file for papers that you are waiting for an answer on so they don't stay piled up on your desk.

- [ ] Make sure you have adequate lighting in this space.

 TIPS:

- Be aware of the traffic patterns in your office and do not block them.

- Don't place your computer screen in front of a window or you will end up with a glare on the screen.

- Cut down on the number of pens, pencils, markers, paper clips, rubber bands, and so on that you keep at your desk so you can use your space for important items.

NOTES:

_____

_____

_____

_____

✔ STAY ORGANIZED!

Once a Week

☐ Input information from loose pieces of paper and sticky notes on your desk.

☐ Clear your "To File" bin.

Once a Month

☐ Clear off your desktop and dust it. Evaluate everything before you put it back on your desk.

☐ Dust your computer and wipe down your keyboard.

Every 3–6 Months

☐ Evaluate your project files and purge those you no longer need. Move completed project files off of your desktop and into a file cabinet.

Once a Year

☐ Go through your files and toss any that you no longer need. Shred any documents with personal information on them.

☐ Update the personal photos you keep at your desk, especially if you have your children's school photos at your desk.

Organize Your Shared Resources

Sharing workspaces and resources can be a tricky situation. Each person has his or her own work style, quirks, and personality. It is important to establish rules that everyone can follow. Having specific homes for items is especially important when multiple people use the same resource. These homes help everyone find what they are looking for right away without looking in several places. Setting rules also makes it easier for new employees to enter the space.

✔ THIS WEEK'S GOALS:

☐ If it has not been done before, hold a meeting with all employees who share the space to discuss systems that can be implemented for sharing resources.

☐ Schedule a day when employees can work together to eliminate clutter. Assign areas of the space so people are not too crowded. Then go through the sorting-and-tossing process.

☐ If more than one employee is sharing a workspace at the same time, consider splitting the space into zones. Zones give everyone enough space to work, help establish a home for everything, and make cleanup easier.

☐ Establish a home for every single item and keep like items together. Clearly label these homes so no one forgets where to put things or find things.

☐ Create a sign-out sheet for resources such as files, disks, and binders that leave the shared space. Clearly label each resource with a specific name. The sign-out sheet should include spaces

> Here is a simple, rule-of-thumb guide for behavior: Ask yourself what you want people to do for you, then grab the initiative and do it for them.
>
> —*MATTHEW 7:12*
> *(THE MESSAGE)*

for the name of the resource, the name and contact information for the person who is using it, the date the item was checked out, and the date the item was returned.

- [ ] Set a time limit for how long shared resources can be kept by an individual and post this time limit on the sign-out sheet.

- [ ] Establish one supply room for *all* supplies. Identify who is responsible for replenishing supplies when they get low.

- [ ] Post a reminder such as "Always put away things before you leave."

 TIPS:

- If numerous employees share a space for working on projects, give each employee his own box or bin and his small inventory of supplies. All items should be labeled with the employee's name.

- If you have an extensive filing system, it may be easier to have one in-box where employees put files when they are done and an assistant who is responsible for refiling.

- If you are working with someone else on a project, have a dry erase board in the space to leave a note of where you left off and where your partner can begin.

✓ STAY ORGANIZED!

Once a Month

☐ Check the shared resources for missing files, disks, etc., that weren't properly signed out.

☐ Straighten up the work area and make sure things are in their proper homes.

Every 3–6 Months

☐ Schedule time to reorder any supplies that are getting low.

☐ Spend a few minutes with new employees to go over the systems that are in place.

Once a Year

☐ Replace old labels that have faded or no longer stay in place.

☐ Hold a meeting to review the systems in place for sharing resources and workspace. Discuss what is working and what is not working. Brainstorm ways to increase efficiency.

NOTES:

_____

_____

_____

_____

_____

_____

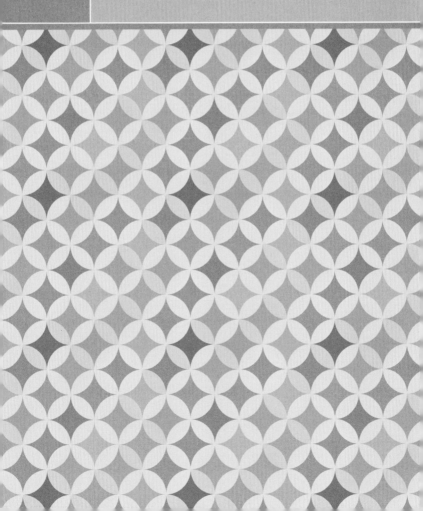

Organize Your Own Business

Organize Your Business Plan

It's a very exciting time when you finally commit to starting a new business. Your best first step to running a successful business is to take the time to write down a specific business plan. Don't worry about making your plan perfect the first time you write it. Start with a rough draft and continue to improve it over time. You can't build on your ideas until you have them all written down. Add and remove things as your plan becomes clearer. This week will give you the framework for writing your plan and will point you to numerous resources that can help you. A good business plan includes four sections:

- Product/Service Analysis and Pricing
- Market Research/Return on Investment (ROI)
- Financing Options
- Long-Term Goals

✔ THIS WEEK'S GOALS:

☐ Decide on a name for your business. I once owned a retail store. I brainstormed and came up with about thirty different names. Then I surveyed family, friends, and my e-mail list for their votes and suggestions. Finally the name Berry Patch Kids was born.

☐ Describe the mission of your business in the opening executive summary. This should be about two paragraphs long.

☐ Describe what your product/service is and what it does.

☐ Describe your pricing strategy.

☐ Describe what kind of image you want to have: convenient, fast, high quality, inexpensive but good, exclusive, etc.

*Choose a job you love,
and you will never have
to work a day in your life.*

—CONFUCIUS

☐ List each of the benefits and features of your company that you will emphasize.

☐ Describe your target market. Who are your customers? Will you target these customers by product line? A geographic area?

☐ Describe important economic factors that will affect your product such as trends, rising prices, industry health, etc. Also list new legal factors and laws that will affect your market.

☐ List each of your competitors including the number of years they have been in business, their market share, their price/strategy, and their product/service features and benefits. Spend time visiting and patronizing your competition. Include both
- Direct competition: companies offering products or services like yours that the customer perceives as an acceptable alternative
- Indirect competition: companies offering products or services different from yours but that meet a similar or same need

☐ List all of your strengths and weaknesses compared to your competitors. Consider your location, reputation, services, employees, size of resources, specialties, price, product features, and operational efficiencies.

☐ Compare your product/service to your competition. What advantages does yours have? What disadvantages does it have?

☐ Discuss how you plan to grow this business. How will you handle setbacks?

☐ List a reasonable timeline that clearly states each of your goals for this business and a time frame for completion of each.

☐ For the first year, create a detailed monthly plan and schedule for running your business. Then create quarterly plans for each year following.

☐ If you will hire employees, include an organizational chart that shows the reporting structure and job description of each employee.

☐ Spend a lengthy amount of time researching your financial options. Clearly list these options and show how much money is needed to make this dream a reality. Tell when and how you will use the funds. Compare your findings with other businesses in your industry.

 TIPS:

- Don't put highly proprietary information into your business plan if others will be reading it.

- Research industry trends to provide facts that can support your claim for your company's potential success.

- Use accurate numbers when describing the size of your target market. To find data on this, visit the U.S. Census Bureau at www.census.gov.

- Make your own investment in your business before going to a potential investor. Many loan programs require a minimum of 20 percent toward any funds sought.

- Focus on growing one aspect of your business at a time. Work on this area until you are successful, and then move on to the next area of improvement.

- Check out these websites for additional assistance in creating your business plan:

    The Planning Shop, www.PlanningShop.com

    Association of Small Business Development Centers,
    www.asbdc-us.org

    National Association of Small Business Investment Companies,
    www.nasbic.org

    Edward Lowe Foundation, www.edwardlowe.org

    National Association for the Self-Employed, www.nase.org

    National Association of Women Business Owners,
    www.nawbo.org

✔	STAY ORGANIZED!
	Once a Month
☐	During your first year of business, review your monthly schedule to make sure you are on track.
	Every 3–6 Months
☐	Review your progress for the previous quarter.
☐	Forecast for the new quarter.
	Once a Year
☐	Update your plan for the upcoming year as needed based on your performance in the previous year and on market/industry trends.

Organize Your Publicity & Marketing Efforts

Marketing means making potential customers aware of your product (or service), and then making them want your product so you can, in turn, sell it to them. Before you can put together an accurate marketing plan, you need to spend some time doing your homework. Find out who your target audience is. Talk to your existing clients. This is one of the best ways to find out who is buying your product or service.

✔ THIS WEEK'S GOALS:

☐ Write down clear objectives for your marketing campaign. What do you hope to accomplish with your marketing plan? Identify how you will measure its success.

☐ Begin to form your marketing plan. Here is an outline for what you should include in your plan:

- **Executive Overview:** Your business's mission, what you stand for, what you hope to provide.

- **Market Review**
    a. Trends
    b. Market Segments: You cannot be all things to all people, so target specific segments of your market and aim to please them. Finding this niche is your key to success.
    c. Target Market: It doesn't matter what you're saying if you're not saying it to the right people!

- **Competitive Review:** Include competing businesses you face as well as product variations you are competing with. Describe each competitor's strengths, weaknesses,

If you take a detour or two, it will not hurt your prospects ... Detours and side trips will add depth to your abilities—and your career—in unexpected ways. Slow down and it will all come together.

—JEAN CHATZKY

pricing structure, marketing campaign, etc. Knowing this information will help you find a unique position for your product.

- **Product and Business Review/PEST:** Political, Economic, Social, and Technological Factors. Describe specific information about your product (or service):
    - a. Its purpose
    - b. The features and benefits
    - c. Pricing structure
    - d. Current distribution channels
    - e. Positioning within the market
    - f. Current advertising and promotions
    - g. Packaging

- **Goals and Objectives**
    - a. Sales Objectives: Set high goals and set a specific timetable to reach these goals.
    - b. Marketing Objectives: These are the ways you will reach your sales objectives.

- **Strategies/Marketing Mix**
    - a. Product
    - b. Price: Consider what your competition charges, what you have to earn to make a profit, and the value of your product.
    - c. Place (also referred to as distribution): Think of this as the "place of purchase." When deciding on

where to sell, keep your product's image in mind and make sure your product will get the attention it needs there.

    d. Promotion: This includes advertising, public relations, direct marketing, promotions/events, company marketing materials, and sales force.

- **Action Plan and Implementation**
  - a. Media Plan: This includes advertising, social media, web promotions, and press releases.
  - b. Budget: Set your budget based on your goals and objectives.
  - c. Schedule: Set deadlines for when each step of the plan needs to be completed and stick to them.

- **Evaluation**
  - a. Establish a tracking system for your leads.
  - b. Review sales figures after a campaign.

☐ Brainstorm. Include other people if you can, and don't shoot any idea down until the end.

☐ Once you've created your marketing plan, order any promotional materials you need.

☐ Set up a "News" or "What's New" page on your website, and link to your media ads or any newspaper articles your company appears in. Update this page regularly to keep it relevant.

TIPS:

- Many times people perceive a product's value based on its price.

- There are two parts of a public relations plan: what you want to communicate and a hook to make it interesting and memorable.

- For most businesses, the magic number for promotions that work is two. Try not to do the same promotion more than twice.

- Don't sell, educate! The key to success is building relationships and helping customers get to know your brand.

✔	STAY ORGANIZED!
	Once a Month
☐	Add to your "What's New" page on your website or blog.
	Every 3–6 Months
☐	Evaluate your marketing efforts from the quarter and compare them to your sales figures to see where you had success.
☐	Reorder any marketing materials that you are getting low on, including business cards.
	Once a Year
☐	Revisit your publicity and marketing efforts from the past year. Make a list of what worked and what didn't. Brainstorm new campaigns. Remember, most promotions only work twice.
☐	Consider taking a college course on marketing or publicity.

Organize Your Business Accounts

The responsibility of record keeping is a hard task for small business owners because this is not their only job. They have many other roles and responsibilities such as meeting with clients, marketing their business, maintaining promotional materials, and hands-on work. With all the daily tasks required to run a business, it comes as no surprise that record keeping is usually the number one thing business owners are behind on.

✔	THIS WEEK'S GOALS:

☐ Designate one home for all of your business receipts and invoices. This information must be kept separate from your personal accounts.

☐ Set a time every week to handle your receipts, invoices, and transactions so they don't pile up. If possible do this work on the same day at the same time every week so you always keep that time open and don't schedule other work.

☐ Discuss with your accountant the best system for processing the transactions that take place in your business. If you do not currently have an accountant, ask for referrals from other small business owners and interview several to find the right fit.

☐ Set an appointment with an accountant to find out everything you need to include in your books. Questions may include:
- How do I pay myself—a salary or a draw?
- Do I have to collect sales tax? How do I do that?
- How can I reduce my taxes? What is deductible?
- What is the best bookkeeping method to use?

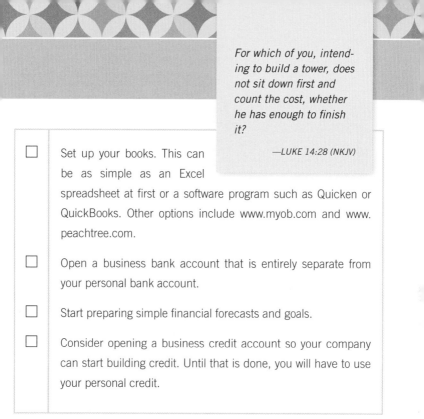

> *For which of you, intending to build a tower, does not sit down first and count the cost, whether he has enough to finish it?*
>
> —LUKE 14:28 (NKJV)

- [ ] Set up your books. This can be as simple as an Excel spreadsheet at first or a software program such as Quicken or QuickBooks. Other options include www.myob.com and www.peachtree.com.

- [ ] Open a business bank account that is entirely separate from your personal bank account.

- [ ] Start preparing simple financial forecasts and goals.

- [ ] Consider opening a business credit account so your company can start building credit. Until that is done, you will have to use your personal credit.

 TIPS:

- Keep up with your filing and paperwork so you can easily find receipts and invoices when you need them.

- Make sure all accounts are reconciled before you print reports.

- Do not waste time billing customers. Get those invoices out so you can get the money in!

- Put aside a little cash into savings every month. When you own a business, your income fluctuates, so you want to be prepared.

✔ STAY ORGANIZED!

Once a Month

☐ Take time to handle and record all of the receipts, invoices, and bills that came in from your business. File them away properly. If this is hard for you, set aside one morning or afternoon a month to do nothing but file.

☐ Review your books.

Every 3–6 Months

☐ If you have a bookkeeper for your business, schedule a meeting to make sure accounts are on track and transactions are being handled accurately and are meeting your standards.

☐ Review your profit/loss for the quarter.

☐ Compare your expenses to your budget, and your income to your forecast, and make adjustments for the upcoming quarter.

Once a Year

☐ Meet with your accountant to discuss taxes for the year and ways to improve the accounts for your business in the upcoming year.

☐ Treat yourself to a fun day or reward at the end of each fiscal year. Running a business is hard work and you deserve it.

Organize Your
Personal Finances

Organize Your Bill-Paying System

Late charges, bad credit, and stress are just a few things you avoid by having an organized system for paying your bills. Organizing an efficient system for paying your bills will not eliminate the sting of money being deducted from your account, but it will buy you peace of mind that your future is a little more secure. And you will save time that can be spent on more enjoyable tasks. Change your attitude about money and you can change your future.

✔ THIS WEEK'S GOALS:

☐ Gather all of your bills and decide on one place to keep them. Whether you are storing them in a file, a basket, or a bin, make sure you have enough room for them. Sort them in a place where you are comfortable working.

☐ Make a list of all of your monthly bills. Next to each bill, write the due date. Then mark these due dates in your calendar or day planner so you don't forget. If the due dates are the same each month, enter them in each month for the year.

☐ Compare your bill due dates to your pay schedule. If possible, see if you can have your due dates adjusted so they coincide with your pay schedule.

☐ Consider your best option for paying your bills. You can always do it the old-fashioned way and mail a check, but you will save time and money (on postage) by paying online. Some companies will also let you sign up for automatic deduction, and you'll never worry about missing a payment or accruing a late fee again. However, you must regularly maintain the balance in your

As you replace old financial habits with new ones, you'll start to feel better about yourself and your ability to take good care of your financial health.

—CHERYL RICHARDSON

checking account if you use this option, or you'll run the risk of overdrafts. The money is deducted from your account whether you have it or not, and it may not always be deducted on the exact same day each month. If you use this option, try to coordinate your due dates with your pay schedule.

☐ Schedule time in your planner when you will pay your bills. The best way is to pay them as soon as you get paid, before the money is spent on something else.

☐ After you pay your bills, write or stamp *Paid* on them and include the date, amount, and method of payment, and place them in a basket or folder until the end of the month. At the end of the month, punch holes in them and file them in a large three-ring binder. Use dividers to mark each category. Or place them in categorized files in your filing drawer. If you pay all of your bills online, always export your receipts and save them in a file in your e-mail or on your computer so you have proof of payment.

☐ Prioritize your accounts. The account with the highest interest rate should be the one you focus on paying off first. If the rates are close, pay smaller balances off first so you have fewer bills to pay each month.

☐ Set goals now for when you would like to have each balance paid off and do your best to meet those goals.

TIPS:

- Use automatic deduction only for bills that are the same amount each month to avoid a surprise overdraft by a higher-than-normal bill.

- If 20 percent of U.S. households paid their bills online, it would save 1.8 million trees a year.

- Sign up for an e-mail or text alert with your credit card company to notify you when you are getting close to your credit limit or billing due date.

- Take the time to read over each of your loan statements. Lenders are required to list how long it will take to pay off your balance with minimum payments. The statement will also list how much you need to pay monthly to settle your balance in three years.

- If your bank does not offer online bill paying, try using a service such as www.mycheckfree.com, which is a highly rated, free bill-paying site.

- If your utility company offers it, consider signing up for an even billing program.

- Call your lenders to see if there is any way they can lower your interest rates. If your lender will not lower your rates, look into transferring your balance to another company. Read everything thoroughly so you are positive that it is a better deal. Be very clear about balance transfer fees and limited-time offers.

- Always read your credit card statements to catch any unauthorized charges.

✔ STAY ORGANIZED!

Once a Month

☐ Pay your bills.

☐ File any statements that you need to save.

☐ Read your credit card statement.

Every 3–6 Months

☐ Shred any statements that you no longer need.

Once a Year

☐ Sort through your filed bills and keep the end-of-the-year statements for investments, credit cards, retirement accounts, or college accounts. Toss all the rest.

NOTES:

_____

_____

_____

_____

_____

_____

_____

_____

_____

_____

_____

Many people avoid organizing their checkbooks or debit card accounts until there is a problem. A disorganized checkbook makes it easy to overspend, which will result in overdraft fees and poor credit. Maintaining your checking account ledger puts you in direct control of your hard-earned money. It also lets you see your daily spending habits and shows you where you can cut back in order to save more money. The easiest way to maintain your checking account ledger is to update it on a scheduled basis, such as once a week. A few minutes a week will allow you to know exactly how much money you have in your account, and you can easily evaluate your statement as soon as it arrives.

✔ THIS WEEK'S GOALS:

☐ Determine the last time you updated your checkbook ledger and then gather all of your bank statements from the present back to the date of your last update. If you only receive electronic statements, export all of the necessary ones to your computer's desktop for easy access. Gather all of the ATM and debit card receipts you can find for this time period, along with the carbon copies of your checks and your deposit slips.

☐ Place all of the receipts, deposit slips, and checks in chronological order, starting with the most distant and ending with the most recent. Enter all of these figures in your ledger—whether it's a software program or a traditional paper ledger.

☐ Place your statements in chronological order and compare them to your ledger. In your ledger, place an X next to each figure that

The greatest good you can do for another is not just to share your riches, but to reveal to him his own.

—BENJAMIN DISRAELI

matches the statement. On the statement, highlight any debits that you don't have receipts for. Enter these into your ledger as well. Circle debits that you don't remember making. If it is a joint account, ask the other party on the account if he or she made those purchases. If it seems fraudulent, investigate further.

☐ Calculate your balance in your ledger and record it. Subtract any bank fees and deposits that have not cleared yet from your total. Add in any checks that have not cleared and any interest you have earned. Compare the final figure to your bank statement. Be sure to contact your bank with any questions or discrepancies.

☐ Now that your ledger is up-to-date, you can create a system to maintain it. Start by finding a secure place to keep all of your ATM and debit card receipts until you enter them in your ledger. This could be in your wallet or in a small coin purse you carry with you. Make it a habit to always put your receipts in your determined place so you don't lose them. If you have a joint checking account, be sure the other party has a method of collecting receipts.

☐ Once a week, input all of your receipts into your ledger or software program (be sure to collect receipts from the other party on your joint checking account). Also include any checks you wrote during the week. Schedule this time in your day planner. If you do it every week, it should take less than fifteen minutes. This is an easy task to do in front of the TV. After you input these numbers, you likely can verify them online and confirm your current balance. You can dispose of the receipts after you input them or keep them in an envelope until the statement arrives and you verify the figures.

☐ Review your statements on a regular basis. You can complete this task during your regularly scheduled weekly register update. Compare it to your ledger or software. Add any service fees and interest accrued into your register. The ending balance on your statement + total of outstanding credits – outstanding debits = your current balance. You can likely verify this on your bank's website.

 TIPS:

- Keep all of your receipts—cash, credit, and debit—in one place. It could be your wallet or a small pouch you carry in your purse. Empty your receipt holder once a week and process the receipts appropriately (record, file, or toss).

- Receipts that require action should go on your to-do list.

- If you are prone to overdrafts, ask your bank if you can set up an e-mail or cell phone alert so your bank will notify you when your account balance is getting low.

- If you can afford it, set up an extra account to back up your main account in case of an overdraft.

- Avoid ATM fees by using your own bank's machines or buying something small at a store and asking for cash back. Also research banks that waive ATM fees altogether.

✔ STAY ORGANIZED!

Once a Month

☐ Review your bank statements and reconcile your accounts.

Every 3–6 Months

☐ Discard any statements and receipts that you have already reconciled and no longer need to keep.

☐ Evaluate your spending habits. Are there simple things you could cut out in order to save money (such as packing a lunch instead of going out every day)?

Once a Year

☐ Don't wait until your debit card is so worn out you cannot use it. If your debit card is getting too worn out, contact your bank to send you a new one.

☐ Get a new check register if you need one. If you use a software program to track your checking account, check for updates or purchase a new program if needed.

NOTES:

_____
_____
_____
_____
_____
_____
_____

Organize Your Budget

A budget is a tool that tracks all of your spending. There's nothing to fear about a budget, and they aren't restrictive. They are empowering. They put you in complete control of your money. When you set a budget and stick to it, you know exactly where all of your money is going.

Budgets are made up of fixed and variable expenses. Fixed expenses are those that are the same amount each month. Variable expenses are those you can control. Any income you have left over after fixed and variable expenses are covered is discretionary money.

✔ THIS WEEK'S GOALS:

☐ Calculate exactly how much income you (and your partner) bring home each month. Know your gross income (pretax and benefits) and your net income (the amount on your paycheck after taxes and benefits have been deducted). Base your investing plan on your gross income. Base your household budget on your net income.

☐ Record your fixed expenses in your expense tracking notebook. If your utilities are not on a even billing plan, gather your bills from the last twelve months and calculate the average monthly cost. Your fixed expenses should be no more than 65 percent of your income. If they are higher than 65 percent, determine ways to lower them.

☐ Track every purchase you make this week. Keep all of your receipts (even if you pay cash) and record them in a notebook at the end of the day. Then write down how you feel about these purchases. After the week is up, add up how much you've spent.

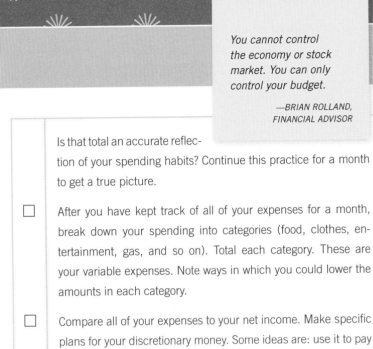

You cannot control the economy or stock market. You can only control your budget.

—BRIAN ROLLAND, FINANCIAL ADVISOR

Is that total an accurate reflection of your spending habits? Continue this practice for a month to get a true picture.

☐ After you have kept track of all of your expenses for a month, break down your spending into categories (food, clothes, entertainment, gas, and so on). Total each category. These are your variable expenses. Note ways in which you could lower the amounts in each category.

☐ Compare all of your expenses to your net income. Make specific plans for your discretionary money. Some ideas are: use it to pay down debt faster, increase your 401(k) contribution, set up a 529 savings account for your child's education, create a dedicated savings account for emergencies, or save it for a near-future goal. It's your money—put it to good work.

☐ Lower your variable expenses by creating a "fixed" cost for each category. Set a specific, realistic limit on how much you can spend per category per month. Carry those numbers with you as you shop and keep track of your spending so you don't go over. If you want to make a purchase bigger than your category budget, save that category money until you have enough to buy it outright. Don't borrow money from future months.

☐ Go through your variable expenses and identify convenience items—things you could do or make yourself for much cheaper. If you rely on convenience items, evaluate your schedule. Could you budget your *time* better to make room for these tasks (e.g., fixing dinner, cleaning your home, etc.)?

TIPS:

- Don't shop when your emotions are high.

- There are lots of great software programs and websites that can help you organize your finances. Try www.mint.com.

- Try to spread your bills out throughout the month. If all of your due dates are too close together, call your lenders or utility companies to see if they can change your due date.

- Make an effort to start giving quality, not quantity, for special occasions and holidays. Just because something is more expensive doesn't mean it will mean more to the person receiving it.

- Budget yourself for seasonal bills such as holiday shopping, vacation, back-to-school, and high heat bills.

- Build credit by paying for groceries and gas with a credit card and paying off the balance every month.

- If charitable giving is a priority, be sure to make room in your budget ahead of time. All contributions to any 501(c)(3) designated organization are tax-deductible. The Better Business Bureau Wise Giving Alliance at www.charitynavigator.org or www.bbb.org/us/charity can help you find legitimate charities that will best fit your values.

NOTES:

STAY ORGANIZED!

Once a Month

☐ At the end of the month, review your spending. What do you regret? How would you spend differently? Keep this in mind when the new month begins and try not to make the same mistakes.

☐ Think about something you can give up this month that will add a minimum of twenty-five dollars to your savings account.

☐ Review your big purchase wish list. Determine how you will save money for these items.

Every 3–6 Months

☐ Plan early for holiday shopping. Set your budget, decide what you will buy each person, and then watch prices on these items and pick them up when you see a deal.

Once a Year

☐ Adjust your budget to reflect any changes in your income.

☐ Adjust any changes in your fixed essential spending to your budget.

☐ Plan ahead for your holiday spending by writing down what you spend during a particular holiday season and hanging on to it for next year.

☐ Sit down with your family to discuss financial goals for the upcoming year and implement any necessary changes to your budget.

Organize Your Emergency Saving Plan

It is always important to have an emergency nest egg set aside, but with the currently high unemployment rate, it's more important than ever to set aside money while you have a job.

Did you know that it typically takes a year from the time you first apply for workers' compensation to receive payment? You cannot rely on that to pay your monthly bills, which means you need to set up an emergency nest egg.

Plus, any number of unfortunate events could cause you financial misery if you aren't prepared—a car accident, natural disaster, medical emergency, broken appliances, etc. Carrying good insurance is wise and can help to an extent, but you will still need to pay the deductible.

The rule of thumb is to save enough for six months of essential expenses, which are housing costs, minimum transportation and childcare, utilities, and food (simple meals cooked at home, not fine dining). If you plan to maintain your current lifestyle without changing your spending habits, you'll need to save more.

✔ THIS WEEK'S GOALS:

☐ Decide whether you are going to pay off your debt before you create an emergency savings account. Many experts say this is the way to go, but others disagree. Think about what is best for your family and job situation. One important consideration is that you will need to save less money to cover six months' worth of expenses if you pay off your debt because you won't need to include debt payments in your emergency fund.

☐ Shop around for a savings account with the highest interest rate you can find. Check out sites such as www.ingdirect.com and

Fear is a poison for which you have an antidote, but you don't know it yet. The antidote is knowing how strong you are, how much you can handle, how you bend but do not break no matter how difficult the things around you become.

—KITTY KOLDING

www.smartypig.com to compare rates. Don't put your emergency fund into CDs or other accounts where your money has to be tied up for a specified time or you face penalties. In an emergency you need cash on hand.

☐ Be realistic about how long it will take you to create your emergency fund. Trying to save this amount of money can be an overwhelming task, so start small. Decide how much you can afford to save out of each check and make the deposits every time you are paid. Or sign up for direct deposit or automatic transfer.

☐ Identify a few items you can cut back on and put all of the money you save by not making these purchases into your emergency fund. Every little bit helps.

NOTES:

_____

_____

_____

_____

_____

_____

_____

_____

TIPS:

- Never put your emergency savings account in your IRA or other retirement account. It would be way too tricky to get the money if you needed it in a hurry.

- Keep your emergency fund in a separate account and make it off-limits for everything but true emergencies. Pulling money from this account should be your last option.

- If you rent your home or live in an apartment, get renter's insurance to cover you in case of a fire or an accident in your home. Your landlord's insurance will not cover your personal property.

An insurance agent can help you understand the differences between the types of coverage available as well as determine what is appropriate for you and your family. Many financial advisors are also licensed insurance agents and can assist you.

Determining how much you should set aside in an emergency fund depends on your personal needs. For a single person, it could be as little as one thousand dollars, which should be enough to cover moderate car repairs or buy an airline ticket if you need to visit someone quickly. If you have a family or large monthly expenses, you should consider a larger amount.

No matter the amount you are putting in your emergency fund, it is best to set up an automatic investment into a separate account so you don't have to think about setting the money aside each month or pay period.

STAY ORGANIZED!

Once a Month

☐ Deposit your budgeted amount into your emergency savings account.

☐ Cut out at least one meal at a restaurant and place the amount you would've spent into your savings plan.

Every 3–6 Months

☐ Schedule regular maintenance for your car to prevent an emergency repair.

☐ Pay your insurance premiums for your home and auto policies.

☐ Schedule regular doctor and dentist visits to avoid emergency procedures.

Once a Year

☐ Review your insurance policies and shop around for better rates.

☐ Schedule a routine physical to screen for preventable medical problems.

☐ Look for ways to lower your everyday expenses and bills, including cable, Internet, and cell phones. The lower your bills, the better off you will be if you have an emergency such as losing your job. You can add these savings to your emergency fund or, if it's fully funded, save for something fun, practical, or your retirement.

Organize Your Financial Goals

By now, we all should know that money can't buy happiness. But let's be honest, the lack of money can bring stress, and stress is, in fact, *unhappiness*. After health concerns, money worries are probably the worst stress a person can have.

Consider working with a financial advisor to set your financial goals. They aren't only for the wealthy. If you make more than ten thousand dollars a year, a financial advisor can help you set goals, pay down debt, and save for your future by giving you an unbiased overview of your personal balance sheet. They set, review, and adjust goals based on market conditions and assist you in navigating volatile markets.

✔ **THIS WEEK'S GOALS:**

☐ Take inventory! Take a very close look at your current financial situation. Be honest with yourself (and your spouse).
- What is your total monthly income?
- What is your total debt?
- What are your assets?
- What is your net worth?
- What cash do you have on hand?
- What could you sell to make money?
- What could you give away?

☐ Set aside time to consider your financial situation. Start by asking these questions:
- What financial steps have you taken lately that are causing you anxiety? Why did you take these steps?
- What are your biggest fears about money?

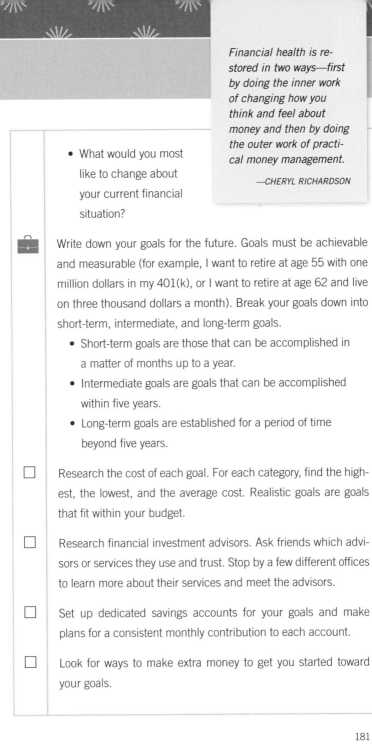

> *Financial health is restored in two ways—first by doing the inner work of changing how you think and feel about money and then by doing the outer work of practical money management.*
>
> —*CHERYL RICHARDSON*

- What would you most like to change about your current financial situation?

Write down your goals for the future. Goals must be achievable and measurable (for example, I want to retire at age 55 with one million dollars in my 401(k), or I want to retire at age 62 and live on three thousand dollars a month). Break your goals down into short-term, intermediate, and long-term goals.

- Short-term goals are those that can be accomplished in a matter of months up to a year.
- Intermediate goals are goals that can be accomplished within five years.
- Long-term goals are established for a period of time beyond five years.

☐ Research the cost of each goal. For each category, find the highest, the lowest, and the average cost. Realistic goals are goals that fit within your budget.

☐ Research financial investment advisors. Ask friends which advisors or services they use and trust. Stop by a few different offices to learn more about their services and meet the advisors.

☐ Set up dedicated savings accounts for your goals and make plans for a consistent monthly contribution to each account.

☐ Look for ways to make extra money to get you started toward your goals.

TIPS:

 Don't sacrifice saving for an emergency fund or retirement in order to pay off debt. When you budget, always include contributions to your retirement fund and contributions to an emergency fund in addition to paying down your debt.

 Your biggest financial goal should be to make certain you do not have a mortgage or any other large amount of debt (e.g., college tuition) when you reach retirement age.

 Review your personal investment portfolio at least on a quarterly, biannual, and annual basis alongside your financial advisors. You may receive a monthly statement, but, generally speaking, monthly reviews can lead to over analyzing the numbers and too much adjustment to the portfolio. Unless market conditions warrant, most advisors would tell you that changing the portfolio monthly would not be a prudent measure.

- Don't make financial decisions quickly, irrationally, presumably, or ignorantly. Take your time and get the facts before you commit.

- Live within or below your means. Be realistic about what you can afford. Get the best quality you can while staying within your means.

- Look for little expenses you can cut from your budget in order to save more. For example, you could put your weekly coffee or pizza money toward your vacation or education fund instead.

- Express gratitude for whatever you have. There is always someone less fortunate. Most of the world's population lives on less than two dollars a day.

✔ STAY ORGANIZED!

Once a Month

☐ Contribute to your dedicated savings accounts.

Every 3–6 Months

☐ Go through your house and look for unused items that you could sell. Put the extra money in savings.

☐ Review your quarterly investment statements and take inventory of your current financial situation.

Once a Year

☐ At the end of the summer, decide where you want to go on vacation next year. Research costs and come up with a twelve-month savings plan to meet your goal.

☐ At the start of each year, decide how much money you want to spend on holiday and birthday gifts for the year. Make a twelve-month savings plan to meet your goal.

☐ Review your investment strategy and asset allocation to accommodate any raises in your salary.

💼 Financial planning is an ongoing process, so review and reassess your plan at least once every year to see what progress you have made and to adjust timetables and goal strategies. This review also gives you the opportunity to plan for changing events or new circumstances that arise from year to year and adjust plans accordingly.

Organize Your Savings

You will never have savings until you first cut down on your debt and, second, you commit to paying yourself! Did you know that you can save ten thousand dollars a year by setting aside only $27.40 per day? Stop and think about this for a minute. In what ways are you spending $27.40 each day that could be used toward this goal? How can you lower your living expenses, including food, housing, transportation, and utilities, to "find" this extra money?

You don't have to save huge amounts of money each year to see the benefits. If you start at age thirty, saving one thousand dollars per year and earning as little as 5 percent interest, you will have more than $126,000 by age seventy.

✔ THIS WEEK'S GOALS:

☐ Shop around at various banks and compare interest rates before you open a savings account. If you already have an account, shop around to see if you can get a better rate. Check out sites such as www.ingdirect.com and www.smartypig.com to compare rates.

☐ Strive to save 10 percent of each paycheck. Remember to always pay yourself first. Make paying yourself easy by setting up an automated plan.

☐ List your savings goals. Beside each goal, write down how much money you will need to achieve this goal and a target to date to reach this goal. Use this information to determine how much money you need to save each month.

☐ Research various investment options, both long- and short-term, that can help you reach your goals. Options include money

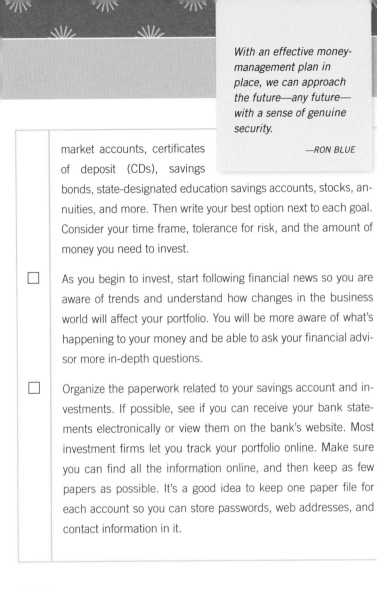

With an effective money-management plan in place, we can approach the future—any future—with a sense of genuine security.

—RON BLUE

market accounts, certificates of deposit (CDs), savings bonds, state-designated education savings accounts, stocks, annuities, and more. Then write your best option next to each goal. Consider your time frame, tolerance for risk, and the amount of money you need to invest.

☐ As you begin to invest, start following financial news so you are aware of trends and understand how changes in the business world will affect your portfolio. You will be more aware of what's happening to your money and be able to ask your financial advisor more in-depth questions.

☐ Organize the paperwork related to your savings account and investments. If possible, see if you can receive your bank statements electronically or view them on the bank's website. Most investment firms let you track your portfolio online. Make sure you can find all the information online, and then keep as few papers as possible. It's a good idea to keep one paper file for each account so you can store passwords, web addresses, and contact information in it.

NOTES:

_____

_____

_____

_____

_____

_____

TIPS:

- If it sounds too good to be true, it probably is. A strong financial plan is the only guarantee for a strong financial future.

- Know the difference between a need and a want.

- When selecting a financial advisor, remember, the bigger the firm, the better the compliance officer watches over the advisors to make sure they are making the right choices for their clients.

- Before you loan money to someone, spend time to think this over carefully. Don't gamble with your security. You have worked hard to save the money you have.

- Consider setting up a separate savings account for short-term goals. For example, you could have one account dedicated to vacations, another to Christmas funds, another to home improvement, and so on. This ensures you contribute to each goal and don't take from one goal to pay for another.

NOTES:

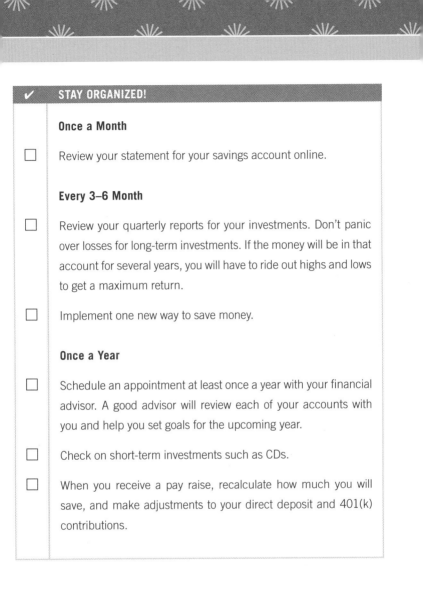

STAY ORGANIZED!

Once a Month

☐ Review your statement for your savings account online.

Every 3–6 Month

☐ Review your quarterly reports for your investments. Don't panic over losses for long-term investments. If the money will be in that account for several years, you will have to ride out highs and lows to get a maximum return.

☐ Implement one new way to save money.

Once a Year

☐ Schedule an appointment at least once a year with your financial advisor. A good advisor will review each of your accounts with you and help you set goals for the upcoming year.

☐ Check on short-term investments such as CDs.

☐ When you receive a pay raise, recalculate how much you will save, and make adjustments to your direct deposit and 401(k) contributions.

Organize Your Children's Finances

In today's world, media and society bombard kids with various messages about money more than ever. It is extremely important that you, as a parent, talk openly with your child and teach them a positive work ethic, strong financial values, and solid money management skills. Teach them the reality of debt and show them how to be wise with credit.

An allowance can be a great tool to teach children money management and basic economic principles. However, if not implemented correctly, an allowance becomes a power struggle if it is used as a reward or punishment or if it lets children assume they can get away without doing chores if they forgo their allowance.

Another way to teach your children about money is to help them start their own business. When I was a kid, my dad had my sister and me sell worms. Although I did not really see the value of this at the time, I have since realized how much we learned by doing this: supply and demand, customer service, inventory control, working hard, the value of a dollar, and so much more!

✔ THIS WEEK'S GOALS:

☐ Identify the purpose of the allowance. Will it only be a reward for chores, or does your child need to do chores regardless? Determine how much allowance to pay each child. Your family's financial situation and your child's age should be the two main influences on this decision.

☐ Set the payday for the allowance. This could depend on when you get paid or when they finish their chores. Whichever the case, make sure that everyone in the family is aware of when payday is.

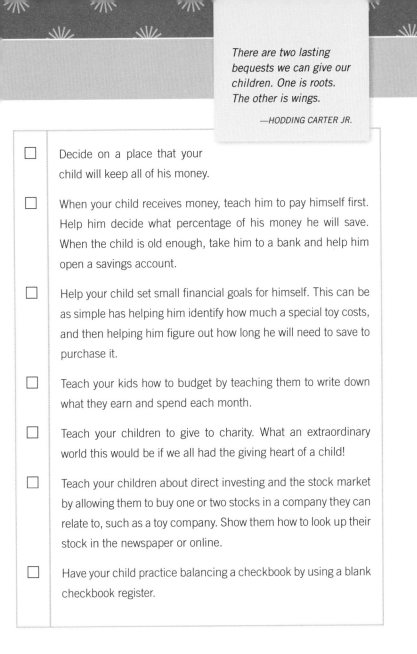

There are two lasting bequests we can give our children. One is roots. The other is wings.

—HODDING CARTER JR.

☐ Decide on a place that your child will keep all of his money.

☐ When your child receives money, teach him to pay himself first. Help him decide what percentage of his money he will save. When the child is old enough, take him to a bank and help him open a savings account.

☐ Help your child set small financial goals for himself. This can be as simple has helping him identify how much a special toy costs, and then helping him figure out how long he will need to save to purchase it.

☐ Teach your kids how to budget by teaching them to write down what they earn and spend each month.

☐ Teach your children to give to charity. What an extraordinary world this would be if we all had the giving heart of a child!

☐ Teach your children about direct investing and the stock market by allowing them to buy one or two stocks in a company they can relate to, such as a toy company. Show them how to look up their stock in the newspaper or online.

☐ Have your child practice balancing a checkbook by using a blank checkbook register.

TIPS:

- *Payday* from Parker Brothers (ages 8 and up) is a great game that teaches kids about money.

- As soon as your child earns an official paycheck, teach her about taxes.

- Allow your children to make minor mistakes with their money. This will help them learn, and it is better that they make mistakes while they are young rather than when they are out on their own.

- Help your child set up a budget *before* he leaves for college. Tell him how he will be accountable for it.

NOTES:

STAY ORGANIZED!

Once a Month

- [ ] Allow your child to spend some of her allowance.

- [ ] Play a fun family game that involves learning money management skills.

- [ ] Have your child look up how much interest his savings account has earned in the past month.

- [ ] Contribute to your child's college savings account.

Every 3–6 Months

- [ ] Encourage your child to make a donation to a charity.

- [ ] Research a business or career with your child either online or at the library. Have the child create a monthly budget based on the average pay for that profession.

Once a Year

- [ ] Review all savings, investment, and college accounts to make sure they are still working for you.

- [ ] Review your allowance policies. Give raises if warranted. The child's birthday is a good time to do this.

Organize Your College Savings Funds

It's no secret that the cost of tuition is rising much faster than inflation. Currently, the average price for four years at an in-state public university is more than fifteen thousand dollars. Four years at a private college is more than thirty-five thousand dollars. It is no wonder parents start thinking about college before their child's first birthday! It doesn't help that we live in a time where families are faced with job loss and plummeting investments. The good news is that there are ways to save money for college, especially if you start saving as early as possible and dedicate time to working for scholarships.

✔ THIS WEEK'S GOALS:

☐ Open a 529 plan for each of your children. These plans offer tax advantages. They come in two forms: prepaid tuition plans, which allow a family to lock into current tuition rates at a participating in-state or private college, and college savings plans, which are invested money that can be used at any school. To find the best 529 plan for your situation, visit www.collegesavings.org.

☐ Decide on an amount you can afford to take from each paycheck to put into a fund for college. Set up an automatic deposit into your 529 plan so saving becomes automatic.

☐ Get an early start on researching any and all possible financial aid that is available to your family, including scholarships. See the tips section for ideas of where to look. When your child starts middle school, look at the qualifications listed for scholarships in your area and be sure your child works toward meeting these qualifications during his or her high school career. Volunteer

It all starts with a dream.
The hardest part is being
willing to do whatever
it takes to make your
dream a reality.

—DAVE THOMAS

work and extracurricular ac-
tivities can be as important as good grades. Start these early so
your child has a long resume to attach to applications.

☐ Look into scholarship programs while your kids are young. You
don't have to be in high school to start getting scholarships! Check
out www.scholarships.com for great information. Kids can get a
scholarship for things like volunteering in their community!

☐ Enroll in a credit or debit card rewards program that gives you
money toward college for your purchases. Friends and family
can even contribute:
  • www.upromise.com: Reward dollars don't expire, and
    they add up (tax-free) until you convert them into checks
    to pay for college expenses or student loans.
  • www.babymint.com: Every dollar in rebates you earn is
    matched by a dollar off tuition at more than 175 partici-
    pating U.S. colleges.

☐ Ask your employer if they offer tuition-assistance programs or
scholarships for dependents as part of your benefits package.

☐ Make an appointment with your child's guidance counselor to sit
down, get advice, and formulate a game plan.

NOTES:

_____

_____

_____

_____

TIPS:

- Women who graduate from college earn 76 percent more than women who have only a high school diploma.

- www.collegeboard.com provides a college savings calculator to help you plan for how much money you need to save.

- www.finaid.org is a free site offering financial aid information.

- www.fastweb.com is a free scholarship-search service.

- www.dosomething.org offers grants and scholarships for socially conscious students.

- Apply for a student loan only after you have explored all of your options for financial aid.

- Set up a college fund as soon as your child is born and commit every penny he or she receives from birthdays, holidays, baptism, graduation, and so forth to this fund. Trust me, this will be way more valuable to your child than yet another toy that will be broken or forgotten in a year.

- Consider completing general studies courses at a community college before transferring to a major college or university. Contact the school to which you plan to transfer to ensure it will accept credits from the community college of your choice. You will only save money if you don't have to retake classes when you transfer.

✔ STAY ORGANIZED!

Once a Month

☐ No matter how small, make a contribution toward your child's college fund.

Every 3–6 Months

☐ Take some time to review the statements for any accounts you have set up for college.

Once a Year

☐ After your child enters middle school, check for available scholarship programs in your area every year. Work with your child's guidance counselors to find these programs.

☐ Research available grants.

NOTES:

_____

_____

_____

_____

_____

_____

_____

_____

_____

_____

Organize Your Retirement Funds

For some people, retirement planning is simply socking away what they can afford, when they can afford to, and hoping for the best. This may be a strategy, but it is not a smart plan. The best thing to do is to paint an honest picture of what you would like your retirement years to look like.

To maintain your current standard of living during retirement, most experts say you will need to have 75 percent of your pretax salary per year. That should be your starting figure when you plan how much you need to save.

✔ **THIS WEEK'S GOALS:**

☐ Work with a financial planner to identify the best retirement savings plan for your goals. Options include:

- A 401(k)
- A Roth 401(k)—the same rules of a traditional 401(k) apply to a Roth 401(k) except you pay taxes on the money before you put it in this account. Then, when you withdraw the money during retirement, the withdrawals are tax-free.
- An Individual Retirement Account (IRA) is a good options for self-employed people or people who don't qualify for a 401(k).
- A Roth IRA

Using a traditional plan allows you to put more money in the account to grow (because you can contribute money that would have gone to taxes). Using a Roth account, however, can help you fit into a lower tax bracket in retirement because money

---

withdrawn from those accounts during retirement is not subject to taxation (because you paid tax on it before you put it in the account).

☐ Let your financial advisor know your target retirement date (even if it's years away), and work with him to set up a portfolio that becomes increasingly more conservative as you approach retirement. When you are ready to retire, the large majority of your funds should be in stable markets so a sudden crash doesn't wipe out your savings.

☐ Look through old paperwork and call or e-mail previous employers to make sure you haven't left money sitting in old 401(k) accounts. If you find old accounts, request paperwork to have the funds rolled into a current qualified account that you are actively managing. Consolidating your money into one account makes it easier to manage and gives you more buying power.

☐ To make it easier to manage your accounts, collect all of your statements and register for online access on each account. Have your quarterly statements e-mailed to you and only save the annual report for tax purposes.

☐ Make sure your beneficiary information is up-to-date on each account.

☐ Compile a list of your assets and have them appraised. Have them properly insured against damage or theft to secure their value.

☐ While you are getting your affairs in order, have your spouse do the same. Then store all of your information in the same spot.

TIPS:

- Regularly contribute to a retirement account (especially a 401(k)), even if you are trying to pay off a lot of debt. Money you save today will be worth so much more than money you save in the future because it will have more time to earn returns on the market.

- Ask your human resources department if you have the option to add money for unused vacation time or overtime pay to your 401(k) account.

- If your company offers a 401(k) match and you haven't take advantage of this, do it today! That is *free* money contributed toward your future!

- Whenever you receive a pay raise, consider continuing to live off your previous pay rate and put the additional funds into your retirement account. At the very least, consider increasing your retirement contribution 1 percent until you reach a minimum of 10 percent.

To save enough money to retire comfortably, save 10 percent of your income annually.

The earlier you start saving for retirement, the better. Individuals who start saving for retirement after age thirty-five have a bigger challenge because they need to save more money in a short amount of time to meet their goal. Those who start later in life will have to be extremely disciplined to make up for lost time.

Try not to come to retirement with all of your funds in only a 401(k) because it will be fully taxable to you when you want to withdraw from it. Consider a Roth IRA if you are eligible.

Once a Month

☐ Make a contribution to your retirement fund. Automatic payroll deduction makes this easy for 401(k)s. If you are contributing to an IRA, be sure to pay yourself and put money in.

Every 3–6 Months

☐ Review your quarterly report for your retirement accounts. Don't panic if you suffered a loss. This is long-term investing, so you need to ride the highs and lows. If you are concerned, discuss it with your financial advisor before you make changes.

Once a Year

☐ Meet with your financial advisor to review your 401(k) and IRA accounts. Make changes if necessary.

☐ Make sure the beneficiary information on all of your accounts is correct.

☐ Review your contribution rates and increase them if possible.

☐ If you are behind in your saving, devise ways you can contribute more this year to help catch up.

NOTES:

_____

_____

_____

_____

Organize Your Cost-Saving Steps

Lately it seems that everyone is looking for ways to save money or be less wasteful with the money they have, which is a very good lesson for us all to learn. And you know what? It doesn't have to be hard to spend less. Here are some ideas anyone can implement.

✔ THIS WEEK'S GOALS:

☐ Organize your belongings on a regular basis to remind yourself how much you already own. The next time you're looking at an item in a store, you'll be able to recall exactly how many similar items you already own before you buy another one.

☐ Start shopping alone. Any parent knows that when you shop with your children, your chances of spending more increase, especially at the grocery store.

☐ Try using only cash while shopping. Leave your credit cards and debit card at home. The cash-only option forces you to stick to your budget. Take a calculator with you to track your spending before you get to the register so you don't have to put items back.

☐ Take advantage of early registration whenever possible. Almost every activity that requires registration will offer a discount if you sign up early enough.

☐ Barter as much as you can! Swap babysitting with a friend. Or swap your talents for another, such as painting in exchange for car repair.

☐ Add your name and birth date to your favorite store's mailing list to get offers on your birthday.

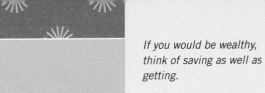

If you would be wealthy, think of saving as well as getting.

—BENJAMIN FRANKLIN

☐ If you are shopping online, try leaving your items in the "cart" for a few days. Some companies will e-mail you a reminder that includes a coupon as an incentive to buy.

☐ Sign up with rebate sites such as www.ebates.com that will refund a percentage of what you spend.

☐ Use the reward programs offered by the stores and gas stations you frequent most often.

☐ Sign up to receive e-mail offers from your favorite stores. You may want to set up a separate e-mail account dedicated to only couponing so sales offers you don't flood your Inbox.

☐ Go to www.energystar.gov and click on Federal Tax Credits to see what upgrades you can add to your house that will save energy and money. Use energy-efficient appliances to help save money.

☐ Give your family a preset number of times you can eat out each month. Have coffee and dessert at home.

☐ Talk online to cut down on your phone plan. If you still need other phone service, research rates at www.calling-plans.com. Find the best cell phone service for you by plugging your account information in at www.billshrink.com.

NOTES:

_____

_____

_____

TIPS:

- Instead of expensive art, display your personal photos on the wall.

- Simmer fresh herbs or cinnamon in water on the stove instead of burning expensive candles.

- Open the door of the dishwasher after the final rinse and let your dishes air-dry.

- Carry reusable water bottles with you to avoid purchasing drinks on the go.

- Grow your own vegetables. If you don't have space for a full-size garden, do your planting in a planter or window box.

- Layer clothing in the winter. This way you can use your spring/summer wardrobe all year.

- Buy and sell your children's clothes at a consignment event in your area. You can earn up to 75 percent of the commission on your sales and also save 50 to 75 percent on buying like-new items!

- Slow down. Every five miles over a sixty-mile-per-hour speed limit costs you ten cents per gallon.

- Save gas by carpooling, using public transportation, and shopping online.

- Run all of your errands at once and organize them geographically so you don't revisit roads you've already been down. You'll save time and money on gas.

- When you set out to buy a vehicle, always settle on the final price before you discuss monthly payments. It is easy for car dealers to jack up the price by giving you a low monthly payment that will take you longer to pay off.

- Ask your doctor to prescribe generic medications whenever possible.

- Use layaway to help you budget your larger purchases or holiday shopping.

- Use PriceGrabber.com, a comparison-shopping site that searches millions of products to help you find the best deals.

- Pack your lunch instead of eating at a restaurant.

NOTES:

Organize Your Couponing

About a year ago, my good friend and business partner turned me on to couponing. Before then I had used about five coupons in my entire life. When she first told me how little she was paying for a tabletop full of groceries, I thought she was lying! I couldn't believe it, so I asked her to teach me how she was doing it. What I learned from her has not only saved me tons of money but tons of time as well! I now enter the grocery store with a firm plan instead of wandering around aimlessly. I also love the convenience of having a well-stocked pantry because I can "shop" from my own shelves and not waste time running to the grocery store for one or two items.

✔ THIS WEEK'S GOALS:

☐ Choose a device for storing your coupons. Here are some options:
  - A three-ring binder filled with plastic sleeves traditionally used to store baseball cards
  - A small file box
  - Small envelopes for each category
  - A mini accordion file that will fit in your purse
  - A large accordion file with coupons left in the inserts

☐ Decide how you will organize your coupons within your storage container. Choose a method that will be easy for you to maintain and easy for you to reference. Here are some options:
  - Sort your coupons by category.
  - Organize coupons alphabetically either by product name or brand name.

> *Get your coupons, learn the ropes, and get organized! Then you gain control and you're in the driver's seat.*
>
> —KRAZY COUPON LADY

☐ Start collecting coupons. You can find them in your local Sunday newspaper, in the stores, on products, direct from the manufacturer's website, and on coupon websites. See the Tips section for specific ideas.

☐ Check the coupon policies and reward programs for your favorite stores by checking their websites, calling them, or stopping by their customer service desk. Find out if and when they will double or triple coupons. Also find out if they offer deals through text messaging.

☐ Search for your favorite brands on Facebook and Twitter, and sign up to receive coupons and promotional information for them.

☐ Track prices on items you buy in a small notebook for the next six weeks. Record prices at different stores. Then look over your data and determine the average price so you'll know when the item is on sale or when you're getting a deal. Also compare prices between the different stores and see which one has the lowest price on the product.

☐ When a product reaches its lowest price (about every twelve weeks), purchase it in bulk. Buy enough of the product to get you through to the next sale (but be aware of use-by dates).

☐ Set up a separate, free e-mail account to use only for coupons and store offers. This keeps spam out of your main account.

☐ Decide on a space for your stockpile.

TIPS:

- You don't always have to buy the exact size product that is mentioned on the coupon. Many times store computers will accept the coupon as long as you are buying the same product listed. Just be sure to watch to make sure the coupon clears.

- Before you go shopping for clothing, electronics, or household goods, do a quick Internet search to see if you can save some money at your favorite stores. Check the store's website. Use a search engine and check the manufacturer's website if you have a specific product or brand in mind.

- Be aware of the use-by dates when you are shopping. There is no sense in buying a product that will expire before you or someone you know can use it.

- Ask family and friends for their coupons from their newspapers if they don't use them. Buy more than one Sunday paper if it is full of great coupons you will use.

- Some reputable coupon sites include:
  - www.smartsource.com
  - www.redplum.com
  - www.coupons.com
  - www.allyou.com

- Pay attention at the checkout! Make sure all of your coupons are scanned and that the correct amount is deducted.

STAY ORGANIZED!

Once a Week

☐ Buy the Sunday paper each week.

☐ Check your favorite coupon websites for the weekly deals.

Once a Month

☐ Go through your stockpile to see if any products are getting close to their expiration date. Make plans to use these products or give them away.

☐ Go through your coupon folder and purge any expired coupons. Make plans to use coupons that expire this month.

Every 3–6 Months

☐ Reorganize your stockpile. Purge expired items. If there are products you just aren't using, stop buying them. Even if you got the product for free, it's a waste of space if you never use it, but likely you paid something for it and you're not getting your money's worth.

Once a Year

☐ Renew your subscription to the Sunday paper.

NOTES:

_____

_____

_____

Organize Your Items for Sale

Selling your unwanted items is a great way to make some extra money while ridding your home of clutter. With one act you can reduce two types of clutter in your life—*stuff* and *debt*! It's a great way to simplify your life, increase your happiness, and decrease your stress. What could be better than that?

✔	THIS WEEK'S GOALS:

☐ Choose a space that can be temporary storage for all of the things you are about to find that you can sell for money.

☐ Go through each room in your home and identify unused, unloved, and unwanted items that you could potentially make money on. Gently used and like-new items will be easier to sell. Move these items to your temporary storage area. Items that have potential resale value include:
- Books, CDs, or movies
- Children's clothing, equipment, and toys
- Collections and antiques
- Furniture and home décor items
- Name-brand clothing and accessories
- China and dishware you never use

☐ Decide how you will sell your items. You have many choices. Here are a few, along with the pros and cons of each:

Consignment Events or Shops

Pro: The shop pays for advertising, and the item stays on sale for sixty to ninety days with no effort on your part.

Con: Items must be in like-new condition, and some shops only accept name brands. Items must be "in season,"

Reduce your clutter. Recycle your like-new items. Reward your family.

—SLOGAN OF MOTHERTIME
MARKETPLACE

meaning you can't sell

a winter coat in July or a bathing suit in December.

Selling on the Internet

Pro: Your items are in front a huge audience. You set the
price.

Con: It can be time-consuming, and fees are costly.

Other considerations: Include a shipping fee in your price.
Consider what percentage the website will take from
your sale. There may be businesses in your area that
will sell items for you online.

Yard Sales

Pro: I'm not a fan of yard sales, so it's hard to think of an
upside to them.

Con: Between the prep work, set up, working the sale,
and tearing down, yard sales are very time-consuming, and you make very little money. You are still stuck
with items that don't sell.

Other considerations: If you plan to have a yard sale,
wait for a community yard sale day in your town or
neighborhood to take advantage of extra traffic and
advertising. If you don't have an organized yard sale
day, see if family, friends, and neighbors would like to
combine their items with yours to have a multi-family
sale that will potentially draw more customers.

Donating

Pro: You automatically get rid of your items. You get a
tax deduction, which will help if you are in a higher tax
bracket and itemize your deductions.

Con: You don't receive actual cash for your goods.

Combining Strategies

Your best bet is to sell your valuable items in a venue that will give you the highest return. If an item is worth less than one dollar to you, donate it.

 TIPS:

- Always clean and repair or iron an item before you sell it.

- Demonstrate that items are in working order. Put fresh batteries in items and have electric items plugged in.

- Research multiple places to donate your items.

- If you have items that you are willing to give away for free, look into bartering sites such as www.mommysavers.com or check out www.freecycle.org.

- If you plan to have a yard sale, price an item as soon as you know you want to sell it, even if the sale is weeks away. Then put it in your designated sales area until the sale.

- If you team up with friends from different neighborhoods, consider moving house to house each week or month until each person hosts the sale. This will give you more opportunities to sell everything!

- If you are selling items, encourage your children to get involved. This is a great way to teach children how to let go of items they are done using and to teach them to earn and save money!

- As soon as you finish decorating for the holidays, look through the unused decorations to see if there are any you can sell.

STAY ORGANIZED!

Once a Month

☐ If you are having trouble selling an item online, consider putting it in a consignment shop or taking it to a business that specializes in online sales.

Every 3–6 Months

☐ Identify at least five unused or unwanted items in your home that you can sell.

☐ Pick up consignment items that didn't sell, or have the shop donate them.

☐ Schedule an appointment with a consignment shop to bring in items for the new season.

Once a Year

☐ Be sure you've received receipts from all of the charities you donated to in the previous year for tax purposes.

NOTES:

Waiting to organize your taxes until tax season is the worst thing you can do! Keep up with it all year by implementing a system now that will work for you. You will save yourself time and possibly money. The most important step you can take to keeping your taxes organized is to first learn what paperwork and information you should and should not be collecting. Do a little research based on your circumstances. It may be best if you speak with an accountant.

The IRS says that audits are computer generated. However, according to accountant Michelle Pohl, some red flags that could trigger an audit include claiming deductions for a home office and claiming a high amount of sales tax.

✔	THIS WEEK'S GOALS:

☐ Designate one place to keep all receipts for the current tax year. It could be a folder, a manila envelope, or a filing system.

☐ When it comes time to prepare your taxes, pull out this folder and make sure all paperwork is sorted into categories:
  - **Income:** W-2, 1099 forms (for interest earned greater than ten dollars), 1099-MISC forms (from any company that paid you more than six hundred dollars), proof of rental property income, dividends
  - **Deductions:** bank and credit card statements, receipts
  - **Medical:** receipts for out-of-pocket expenses if you think you spent more than 7.5 percent of your adjusted gross income
  - **Donations:** receipts for cash and noncash donations (cleared checks are no longer accepted; you must have a receipt)

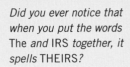

Did you ever notice that when you put the words The *and* IRS *together, it spells* THEIRS?

—*UNKNOWN*

- **Receipts** for child care costs and major home improvements
- **Real Estate:** interest statements from your mortgage, property taxes
- **Tax Correspondence:** letters from the IRS or your state revenue service

☐ If you use an accountant, call to schedule an appointment by the middle of January. If you need an accountant, ask friends and family for referrals. Try www.accountant-finder.com, where you can search by city.

☐ Consider your filing options. If you have a simple return (no deductions), you can consider doing your taxes yourself using a free tax software program (see the Tips for a list). If you use tax software, make sure you have the most recent version. If you do your taxes yourself, complete them before March 1 so you have time to schedule an appointment with a professional if you have problems.

☐ Purge and organize your tax papers from previous years. Keep all records for the past seven years; dispose of any that are more than seven years old. Other basic guidelines for saving tax paperwork are:
- If you are behind in your taxes, keep the paperwork indefinitely.
- Real estate transactions should be kept indefinitely.
- Keep receipts for all major home improvements for as long as you own the home.

TIPS:

- Many companies now offer free online software and systems to help you complete your federal tax forms, but you must pay a fee to complete your state forms with the same system. Some options include: TurboTax, H&R Block's TaxCut, TaxACT, CompleteTax, TaxEngine, and TaxSlayer.

- Checks for charitable deductions are no longer acceptable; you *must* have a receipt from the charity.

- If you donate time rather than money to an organization, you may be able to deduct what is called charitable miles if you drive long distances.

- When building a house, you may be able to claim the sales tax you paid on all building supplies.

- If you are contributing to your child's college tuition, see if you qualify for one of these three ways to deduct your contributions:
    Hope Credit
    Lifetime Learning Credit
    Tuition and Fees Deduction

- If you are self-employed, you may get a dollar-for-dollar deduction if you are currently paying for health insurance.

- Visit www.freefile.irs.gov to see if you qualify for free income tax preparation.

- For answers regarding taxes, go to www.irs.gov.

- Go to www.kiplinger.com for a list of commonly missed deductions.

STAY ORGANIZED!

Once a Month

☐ Go through your desk and office and file any tax receipts that may be lying around. Be sure to check your planner, briefcase, or purse, too.

Every 3–6 Months

☐ Update any Excel sheetsheets, books, or software that you use to keep track of your receipts and deductions throughout the year. Enter all receipts.

Once a Year

☐ Set up an appointment with a tax professional by the end of January.

☐ If you use software to prepare your taxes, make sure you have the updated version that you need. If not, purchase a newer version.

☐ Purge files from the previous tax year. Shred paper such as monthly statements (you only need the last one) and paycheck stubs once you have reconciled them with your W-2 or 1099 forms.

☐ Purge tax files more than seven years old.

NOTES:

_____

_____

_____

Organize Your Insurance Papers

Insurance is a part of everyone's life. Auto insurance is required by law. Homeowners insurance is a condition of having a mortgage. Insurance protects you from the risk of financial ruin due to a number of reasons, so it's very important. Unexpected medical emergencies are one of the main reasons people go bankrupt. Insurance policies come with a lot of paperwork, and most people have multiple policies—home, auto, life, and medical. This week will help you maintain your insurance paperwork so you can get the most from your coverage.

✔ THIS WEEK'S GOALS:

☐ Create separate folders for each type of insurance you have. Categories include health, auto, homeowners or renters, life, and assets.

☐ Gather up all of your insurance papers from around the house and sort them into their specific categories. Then go through each category and keep only your most current policy information. Shred outdated policies and paperwork.

☐ While you are looking through your current policies, check around to see if you could receive a better deal by switching insurance companies or combining multiple policies (such as home and auto) to one company.

☐ Don't pay for insurance you don't need. If you and your family are healthy, opt for a leaner medical policy that covers routine exams and catastrophes. Put the money you save into an account to cover the high deductible. For home and auto, carry coverage

The good news is that it is compelling to keep a workspace open once you have established a system for managing papers. The bad news is that without a system, paper piles up.

—PORTER KNIGHT

that will cover what you owe on the property or what it will cost you to replace it. Don't overpay for extras you don't need.

☐ File all statements of benefits you receive from your medical insurance company. This is your proof that the insurance company has paid its part of the bill for a medical expense.

☐ Create a separate file for all medical claims you are disputing. Keep all communications related to this dispute in this folder. Also include a call log and use it to document calls you made, including the date and time you called, whom you spoke to, and the results of the phone call.

☐ If you make claims against your home or auto insurance, file all paperwork related to that claim in the appropriate folder. If the claim is complicated or includes a lot of disputes and paperwork, create a separate folder.

☐ Place your most important papers in a fireproof safe or safety deposit box. Whenever possible get PDF versions of these documents as backups. They can also be used for a quick, searchable reference. If it is not easy to get a PDF version, scan the original on your home printer and save the image to your computer.

TIPS:

- If you owe medical bills, make a five-minute phone call to the doctor to see if you can get your bill lowered. Many hospitals and doctor's offices will work with you so they can get paid. At the very least, you can always set up a payment plan to avoid getting sent to collections.

- If you lose your job, check out the COBRA law, which allows you to maintain your health insurance through the company you worked for after losing your job. For details go to www.dol.gov/cobra.

- Before paying for any health insurance, check the company's list of providers to make sure there is an in-network provider who meets your needs. Then double-check with the provider to verify that he or she accepts the plan you are considering.

- Find the right insurance agent—one you trust and who will answer your questions and explain things in layman's terms.

- Some insurance companies offer a discount if you pay for your policy in six-month intervals instead of monthly. When possible, take advantage of this discount.

NOTES:

Once a Month

☐ Make your monthly payments on your policies.

☐ Review all statements of benefits as soon as they arrive. Open a dispute right away if needed; otherwise file the statement with your medical insurance papers.

Every 3–6 Months

☐ Get new quotes for your car insurance every six months. Customer loyalty doesn't mean much these days to car insurance companies, so shop around for a better price.

Once a Year

☐ Review your insurance policy before you automatically renew each year. Have your needs changed? Can you save money by switching?

Organize Your Estate

Let's face it, the reason we need to have our estate organized is because we will, in fact, die someday. It's not a fun topic to discuss, but it's part of life and another area we need to properly manage. Think of this project as a gift to those you leave behind because the more you get things in order now, the less chaos will take place when you are gone. By organizing your estate now, you will protect your beneficiaries, reduce the potential for disputes, reduce the amount of taxes your estate will owe, create your legacy, and give yourself peace of mind.

✔ **THIS WEEK'S GOALS:**

☐ Begin drafting a will. You can find will kits online and in bookstores. It's also a good idea to contact your lawyer to see if he or she has a kit. Your will should include the following:
- Your full legal name
- Your address
- A statement that you are of sound mind and that the will is yours
- A clause revoking all previous wills
- The legal name of your current spouse
- The names of all your children, including birth dates for each
- The name of your will executor and the responsibility you are giving him
- The name of each beneficiary and the assets you are leaving each one
- The names of your children's personal and property guardian if you have minor children
- The names and addresses of your witnesses

If life was a blast without pain or sorrow, would we die any better for having lived?

—SANTA MONTEFIORE

☐ Date and sign your will in front of two competent adult witnesses and have your will notarized. Check your state's laws to see if you need you to have all of the signatures on your will notarized or if you just need one notary mark for the will.

☐ Decide who will be your primary and secondary beneficiary on your life insurance policy. Consider who will benefit from your money when you pass away and who will need to pay for your burial services. It is important to select a beneficiary no matter what size your estate is. Doing so will save loved ones from losing intended benefits, lessen legal complications, and hopefully avoid unexpected tax bills. If you do not name a beneficiary, life insurance proceeds will go into your estate and can be subject to estate taxes. A beneficiary can be:

- One or more people
- A trust you've set up
- Your estate
- A charity

☐ Designate a durable power of attorney document. This is the person you select to act on your behalf if you are no longer able to handle your own affairs. This form is available online through your state government.

☐ Complete a medical power of attorney or a living will, which is the official record of the person you select to act on your behalf in regard to medical decisions. This form is available online through your state government.

- [ ] Write or type up a list of all tangible property that is part of your estate. Tangible property includes anything you can hold or touch, including jewelry, vehicles, artwork, furniture, and collectibles. In the first column name the item (be specific), and then put the value next to it.

- [ ] Locate all paperwork that is needed for this inventory, especially any that proves the value of the item, and make a file to safely house these documents. This file may include warranties, receipts, real estate deeds, insurance papers, etc.

- [ ] Keep a copy of your will in a fireproof box in your home, and keep another copy in a safety deposit box at a bank. Keeping a will in two places protects it in the event of a fire.

 TIPS:

- When an estate is worth three million dollars or more, it is time to look at estate planning. Estates in this value range are subject to taxes of 50 percent or more when you die.

- If you name your spouse as your beneficiary and later get divorced, be sure to name a new beneficiary; otherwise your estate could go to your former spouse, even if you remarry.

- Designate a secondary beneficiary on each of your accounts in case something were to happen to your primary beneficiary at the same time that you die. If something happens to your primary beneficiary while you are still alive, update your beneficiaries so you have two eligible beneficiaries at all times.

- Update your beneficiary information after the birth or adoption of a child.

✔	STAY ORGANIZED!

Once a Month

☐ Add major purchases to your list of tangible property.

Every 3–6 Months

☐ If a big life event happens, such as a birth, death, divorce, etc., be sure to make any necessary corrections to your will and beneficiary information.

Once a Year

☐ Review your will to make certain that it is up-to-date and continues to reflect your wishes.

☐ Review your estate planning documents to see if any updates need to be made.

☐ Make sure the beneficiary information on all of your accounts is up-to-date.

NOTES:

Organize the Sale of Your Home

According to Realtor Susan Kautz, the highest amount of traffic occurs within the first four weeks of listing a property on the market, so it's important to price your home right the first time.

The top three things that make a house sell are location, appearance, and price. While you can't change the location, you can improve the appearance, primarily by staging. Staging is the act of depersonalizing a house, in other words, taking the "home" out of a house. This allows buyers to see what they are getting and makes it easier for them to imagine their own family living in this space.

✔	THIS WEEK'S GOALS:
☐	Arrange an off-site storage facility or an on-site rental unit to hold excess furniture and personal items. Don't cram extras you want to hide into closets, basements, attics, or garages. Buyers will look everywhere, and you want storage areas to seem spacious. Loading them up will have the opposite effect.
☐	Repair anything that is broken now so it is not something that will be taken off your asking price later. Be sure to repair any holes in the walls.
☐	Stage an area around the focal point of the room. For example, in the bedroom it would be the bed; in the living room it would be the fireplace or couches.
☐	Remove excess knickknacks from flat surfaces and books from shelves. Remember three is the magic number. Remove all family photos from walls and tables so buyers can picture the house as theirs and not yours.

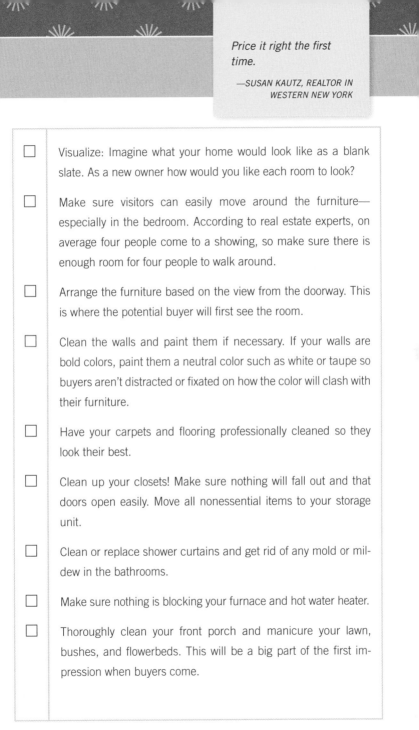

> *Price it right the first time.*
>
> —SUSAN KAUTZ, REALTOR IN
> WESTERN NEW YORK

☐ Visualize: Imagine what your home would look like as a blank slate. As a new owner how would you like each room to look?

☐ Make sure visitors can easily move around the furniture—especially in the bedroom. According to real estate experts, on average four people come to a showing, so make sure there is enough room for four people to walk around.

☐ Arrange the furniture based on the view from the doorway. This is where the potential buyer will first see the room.

☐ Clean the walls and paint them if necessary. If your walls are bold colors, paint them a neutral color such as white or taupe so buyers aren't distracted or fixated on how the color will clash with their furniture.

☐ Have your carpets and flooring professionally cleaned so they look their best.

☐ Clean up your closets! Make sure nothing will fall out and that doors open easily. Move all nonessential items to your storage unit.

☐ Clean or replace shower curtains and get rid of any mold or mildew in the bathrooms.

☐ Make sure nothing is blocking your furnace and hot water heater.

☐ Thoroughly clean your front porch and manicure your lawn, bushes, and flowerbeds. This will be a big part of the first impression when buyers come.

☐	Clean the gutters.
☐	Repair broken steps, decks, porches, or fences.
☐	Add some new potted plants to the entryway if the weather permits.

TIPS:

 Consider a home inspection before you list your home. You will know what to expect and know if you will need to lower the price.

Make sure your house looks well maintained. Vacuum before each showing so buyers can see fresh vacuum marks.

- Be aware of any odors. In the staging industry they say, "You can't sell it if you can smell it." Purchase air fresheners in baking scents, but make sure they are not overpowering.

- When selecting a Realtor, look for a salesperson with a type A personality.

- Look for a Realtor who will give you honest feedback when selling your house. You should expect to hear honest feedback after each and every showing.

- Ask these questions when interviewing a Realtor:
    1. What is your current sales volume?
    2. What are your advertising/marketing capabilities? What is your budget for this?
    3. How much time do you spend in the office? Note: The less time, the better. A good Realtor should spend little time in the office. She should be busy showing and listing property.

| ✔ | **STAY ORGANIZED!** |

☐ **Before a Showing:**
- Make the beds.
- Clean the kitchen sink, countertops, and appliances.
- Remove all hanging laundry or dirty laundry on the floors.
- Vacuum the floors.
- Clean the bathrooms.
- Clear everything out of the showers and tubs except one bottle of shampoo and one bottle of liquid soap.
- Open the shower curtains.
- Flush all toilets and close the lids.
- Remove any sign of pets.
- Make sure all closet doors open easily.
- Sweep the front porch, steps, and walkways.
- Mow the grass.
- Add a fresh vase of flowers to the entryway.

NOTES:

_____

_____

_____

_____

_____

_____

_____

_____

_____

_____

Organize Your Credit Reports

Credit scores range from 300 to 850 (perfection). Ten percent of your score is determined by how well you manage different types of credit. For example, managing a mortgage, credit card, and auto loan at the same time can increase your score if done well. Fifteen percent of your score is determined by your credit history. It can actually hurt you to close an account that has been paid off. Ten percent of your score is affected by recent credit applications. This week's goals will give you valuable advice on how to manage your reports and raise your credit score.

✔ THIS WEEK'S GOALS:

☐ Check your credit reports. You can purchase them directly from the three major credit bureaus: www.equifax.com, www.transunion.com, and www.experian.com. The official site to obtain all three reports for free is www.annualcreditreport.com. You can get a free report:
  - Once every twelve months
  - Within sixty days of being denied credit
  - While you are disputing an account

☐ If there are errors on your credit report, write to each credit company and ask for their assistance in removing these errors and getting issues resolved. If you feel that your identity has been stolen, contact one of the credit bureaus immediately, and they will contact the other two.

☐ Set up an online account with your credit card companies so you can check your statements weekly and respond quickly if someone tries to make fraudulent charges to the account.

We have the choice to live our lives "leading with our strengths," or offering our challenges as excuses for our failures.

—WILMA FELLMAN

☐ Make it a priority to always pay your bills on time. Late payments can affect your credit score for up to four years. A late mortgage payment can knock one hundred points off your score overnight. If you can't make a payment, make arrangements with your lender before the bill goes past due.

☐ Keep balances and limits low on credit cards and other revolving credit lines.

☐ Do not close unused credit cards if you can help it. Likewise, do not open credit cards you don't need in order to try to improve your credit score.

☐ If you have had credit problems in the past, reestablish your credit history by slowly opening accounts and paying off the balances. Keep the balances low enough that you can easily pay the entire bill at the end of the month to avoid interest and debt while building a good payment history. Consider starting with a secured credit card. These accounts allow you to deposit money into an account before you use it.

☐ If you need to shop around for new credit, such as a loan, limit the time of your search to about fourteen days or less. You can lower your score if you have too many inquiries that you initiated.

☐ Educate yourself by reading up on the Fair Credit Billing Act so you know what your credit card company can and cannot get away with. Learn more in the Consumer Protection section at www.fdic.gov.

TIPS:

Employers as well as lenders look at your credit score. A good credit score shows you are responsible, whereas a bad score can mean that you are a less responsible person, and that makes a difference with employers when they are hiring.

- If you find yourself having a hard time paying your bills, consider credit counseling. The National Foundation for Credit Counseling (www.nfcc.org) is a great nonprofit.

- If you are more than sixty days late on your payment, the credit card company can raise your interest rates.

- Don't ever opt for the "right" to go over your credit limit. It can cost you dearly.

- If you are considering consolidation for your loans, do your research and make sure it is really worth it. Enrolling in a credit-counseling program can be noted on your credit report for seven years.

- Spend less time moving debt around and more time paying it off.

- If you need to transfer a balance, look for a fixed promotional rate that will last long enough for you to pay off the balance.

- Installment debt (such as a mortgage) is considered better than having revolving debt like credit cards.

- Never pay a fee to consolidate debt!

- Write your credit card balance on a sticky note and place it on the card to remind you to think next time you have the urge to spend!

- If you need more credit, consider requesting a higher limit from your current lenders rather than opening a new account.

✔ STAY ORGANIZED!

Once a Month

☐ Review all credit card statements when they arrive to verify you authorized all charges.

☐ Schedule time to pay your bills.

Every 3–6 Months

☐ Check on any disputes you have made to the credit companies and make sure they have been resolved and taken off your report.

☐ Evaluate your accounts and reprioritize if necessary.

Once a Year

☐ Visit www.annualcreditreport.com to order a free copy of your credit report.

☐ Immediately call about any issue or misreported information on your report.

☐ Try to get your current credit card interest rates lowered, or look into transferring your balances.

NOTES:

_____

_____

_____

_____

Organize Your Anti-Identity Theft Plan

Identity theft is a devastating crime that will haunt you for years. The worst part is you could be a victim and not even know it. When it comes to protecting your identity, you must be proactive. Limit the amount of personal information you put on the Internet, and only use reputable companies that have secure websites when making an online purchase. Every home needs a shredder to prevent personal information from going out in the trash where it could be collected and used illegally.

Most importantly, monitor your credit reports once a year. If you feel that your identity has been stolen, contact one of the credit bureaus (Equifax, Experian, TransUnion) immediately, and they will contact the other two.

✔ THIS WEEK'S GOALS:

☐ Whenever you receive a new credit card, instead of signing your name to the back of it, write "See Identification." This requires merchants to ask to see your ID whenever you use the card, which means thieves won't be able to use it in stores if they steal it.

☐ Set up a "Fraud Alert" or "Security Alert" on your credit reports. Do this by selecting this choice on your online credit reports or by calling the credit bureaus directly. This alert makes sure banks verify your ID before they extend credit. It only lasts for ninety days but is renewable.

☐ Place your Social Security card in a locked filing cabinet or fireproof safe. Never carry it in your wallet.

☐ Put all credit card offers you receive, bank statements, and investment statements through your shredder. If you don't own a

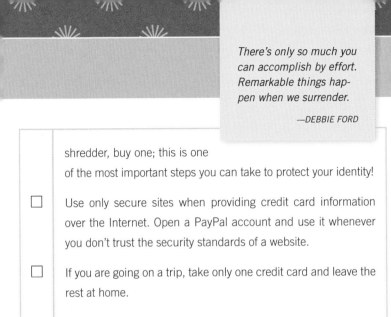

> *There's only so much you can accomplish by effort. Remarkable things happen when we surrender.*
>
> —DEBBIE FORD

shredder, buy one; this is one
of the most important steps you can take to protect your identity!

☐ Use only secure sites when providing credit card information over the Internet. Open a PayPal account and use it whenever you don't trust the security standards of a website.

☐ If you are going on a trip, take only one credit card and leave the rest at home.

TIPS:

- If you are not comfortable giving out your Social Security number as a form of security ID over the phone, ask if there is another form of identification you can give.

- You can forward all spam pop-ups that try to get your personal information to spam@uce.gov.

- If you are disputing a charge on your credit card, you should always follow up a phone call with a letter. Send it via certified mail to receive confirmation when it arrives at the company.

- Always pursue suspected fraudulent charges on your credit card. The law requires bureaus to investigate a disputed item.

- Open your credit card statement every month (or check it online), even if the card has a zero balance, to make sure that someone hasn't made a fraudulent charge to your account.

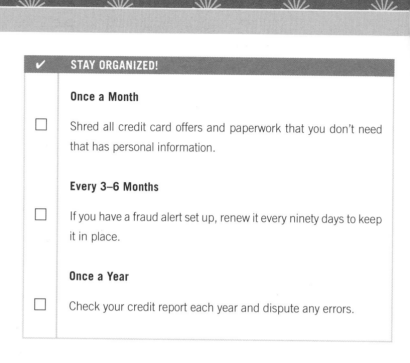

✔	**STAY ORGANIZED!**

Once a Month

☐ Shred all credit card offers and paperwork that you don't need that has personal information.

Every 3–6 Months

☐ If you have a fraud alert set up, renew it every ninety days to keep it in place.

Once a Year

☐ Check your credit report each year and dispute any errors.

NOTES:

234

Index

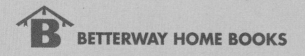

BETTERWAY HOME BOOKS

Find More Helpful Organizing Books

*Organize For a
Fresh Start*
by Susan Fay West

Organized Simplicity
by Tsh Oxenreider

*Organize Now! 12 Month
Home & Activity Planner*
by Jennifer Ford Berry

Available online and in bookstores everywhere!

Organizing Tips e-Book

- Advice from organizing experts Jennifer Ford Berry, Debbie Lillard and Tsh Oxenreider.
- Quick, practical tips that give immediate results.
- Time-managment ideas to maximize holiday fun.

Visit **betterwaybooks.com** to download your free copy.

To get started join our mailing list at **betterwaybooks.com**.

FOLLOW US ON:

*Become a fan of our Facebook page:
facebook.com/BetterwayHomeBooks*

*Find more great advice on
Twitter: @Betterway_Home*